Here's evidence that with God's help all things are possible. These remarkable stories of South Africans who overcome economic, social, and spiritual oppression through faith are testimonies that missionary efforts are bearing incredible fruit. Two thumbs up for a great book.

—Tony Campolo
    author and sociology professor at Eastern University

Most of the success stories we Christians tell each other are inspirational tall tales. Even when the facts are technically true, we ministry people generally edit ourselves in such a way as to dazzle—and raise money. So then, both the good news and the bad news is that Chrissy Jeske's collection of stories about the common, unmiraculous transformations of common, un-miraculous people is both rare and remarkable. If you are looking for some honest hope in a world full of trouble, here it is.

—Bart Campolo
    author, speaker, and leader of the
    Walnut Hills Fellowship

Africa is a rich, harsh, diverse land not made for sissies! In this riveting book Christine Jeske invites you to experience, and possibly wrestle with, the many massive burdens encountered by authentic 21st century Africans. With their few creature comforts and minimal Western luxuries, they draw us into the reality of living out Christ in the midst of trials, tradition, and tribulation. The "mud" of each story in this book forces readers to examine the impact of God's Living Water to cleanse, clarify, and cultivate. This is a book we should all read; it expands the mind and softens the heart.

—Rona Miller
    executive editor of *Christian Living Today*
    (South Africa)

D0061746

God is calling his people to a strange joy, the kind that comes only by borrowing the discomfort of others. Some hear the call; many do not. Christine Jeske hears it and passes it on to us. You don't have to love Africa to hear the invitation. Africa's stories are like all stories in the world's hard places. The invitation is to accompany one another in the pilgrimage of faith.
—MICHELE RICKETT
founder and president of Sisters In Service and coauthor of *Daughters of Hope* and *Forgotten Girls*

God made the first human by breathing into dirt. Jesus healed a blind guy by picking up mud, spitting in it, and wiping it on the man's eyes. Jesus interrupted a death penalty case by drawing in the sand as people dropped their stones, and He told a bunch of religious folks if they want to enter the kingdom of God they need to play in the dirt with the kids. The Scriptures are full of stories of a God who is not afraid of dirt, who is just as likely to show up in the sewers of the slums as in the polished halls of the temples. Christine Jeske has felt the mud between her toes and has seen God at work in the dirt. This is a book of dirty theology. It's about a God who is not scared of getting dirty, and invites us to join Him in the mud. May we have the courage to roll up our pant-legs and follow.
—SHANE CLAIBORNE
activist and author of *Jesus for President*

Into the Mud tells the real stories of Africa. These are not the tragic stories, fairy tales, or classic cliches of many novels. Instead, they are the stories of Africa today—of people struggling to better their lives, of finding hope in God and community. Jeske's openness with her own story invites the

reader into the realities of walking with your neighbor. This book will be valuable to individuals and groups in examining their preconceived notions of development and developing nations, or as they prepare for a cross-cultural experience.
—PAMELA CRANE
water project manager for Blood:Water Mission

Into the Mud is an engaging picture of how to enter another culture from the position of a learner and a fallen human being, but still with a view to bring about positive change. Christine Jeske's carefully chosen, well-written stories all have lessons to be learned and are followed by questions for discussion and reflection. I recommend this book highly for those thinking of cross-cultural ministry, be it short- or long-term.
—JIM TEBBE
Urbana Director

Jeske presents a number of compelling narratives that serve as a powerful reminder that the kingdom of God is not found in worldly comforts and pleasures, but rather in the mundane, anonymous struggles of ordinary people trying to make sense of the complexities of life. Jeske does a wonderful job of navigating through complicated issues of race and class in the developing world in ways that are accessible and personal, and with a distinctively Christian foundation that adds depth and meaning beyond the difficult circumstances described in her accounts. A much-needed example of grace and humility in the way Western Christians respond to global needs.
—MATT KOSCHMANN
assistant professor of communications at the University of Colorado at Boulder

Into the Mud is an adventure from cover to cover! A young mother from Wisconsin rides her motorcycle across the South African countryside, searching for the Africa of which she had dreamed back on her college campus. What she finds instead is more than colorful folktales and exotic music—she finds miracles of faith and God's love at work in the "mud" of extreme poverty, violence, racism, and disease. This book is full of love, hope, and inspiration, and it is sure to launch a huge Christine Jeske fan club. I'm already eager to see her next one!

—DON MOSLEY
founding member of Jubilee Partners and
author of *With Our Own Eyes*

Through raw, honest, careful, and dignified retelling of still-in-process stories of people in South Africa, *Into the Mud* shows how our Creator and Redeemer enters into the pain of people surrounded by injustice in order to provide comfort and strength as these everyday heroes encounter and embrace faith, hope, and love. I was inspired and deeply moved.

—BENJAMIN HOMAN
president of Food for the Hungry

Jeske offers winsome, colorful exhibits of God's grace and Kingdom movement in a landscape of globalized juxtapositions. *Into the Mud* reminds us that indeed, every story is a travel story, as the journey of becoming and hope are inextricably woven together in the faces of everyday people. One need not have traveled to the southern tip of Africa to appreciate a literary arousal of the senses as the author walks the reader through the social and physical topography of the Zulu nation. Of course, if one has traveled to this mountainous region of South Africa, these stories ring with authentic detail and perspective. A wonderful read for anyone who wishes to understand this nook of our planet or who just longs to hear more evidence of God's redemptive work in the muddy places of life.

—GARY T. LAVANCHY
adjunct instructor and discipleship coordinator
at Wheaton College

Beautifully and engagingly written, Christine Jeske brings us deep reflections and poses important questions from the front lines of ministry to the poor in southern Africa. Through a series of sensitively written and evocative stories of ordinary people, a mosaic of Africa as it is today emerges before our eyes—complex, deeply Christian, caring, and humane. The key issues of mission, poverty, development, and justice surface through these compelling lives. This is a book that you must read.

—BRYANT L. MYERS
professor of international development at
Fuller Theological Seminary and
author of *Walking with the Poor: Principles and Practices of Transformational Development*

If Jesus loved to use story in order to teach the crowds, then it is clear that Christine Jeske is surely one of His disciples. *Into the Mud* sings in well-written narrative the glories of God in a context of hardship and joy, suffering and victory. It's one of those books that beg for the page to turn in order to discover what happens next. Christine walks us through the South African dust in dry season and the mud in rainy season, and in the process we discover Christ and His coming kingdom—sometimes with great challenges, but often with rewarding surprises. I urge you to journey with her into the mud and straight to the heart of God.

—SCOTT A. BESSENECKER
associate director of InterVarsity Missions and author of *The New Friars: The Emerging Movement Serving the World's Poor*

Christine wrestles with some of the world's greatest problems but offers glimpses of hope in a landscape of need, seeds of reconciliation in a history of brokenness, and stories of enduring faith in the most unlikely places. Using moving vignettes, Christine Jeske accomplishes what statistics fail to do —plunge us into the grit and reality of the world's largest issues and move us to action. Jeske is a master storyteller and this outstanding book contains stories that need to be told.

—PETER GREER
president of HOPE International and coauthor of *The Poor Will Be Glad*

into the mud

INSPIRATION FOR EVERYDAY ACTIVISTS

CHRISTINE JESKE

TRUE STORIES OF AFRICA

MOODY PUBLISHERS
CHICAGO

© 2010 by
CHRISTINE JESKE

All rights reserved. No part of this book may be reproduced in any form without permission in writing from the publisher, except in the case of brief quotations embodied in critical articles or reviews.

All Scripture quotations, unless otherwise indicated, are taken from the *Holy Bible, New International Version®*. NIV®. Copyright © 1973, 1978, 1984 by International Bible Society. Used by permission of Zondervan. All rights reserved.

Some names and minor details have been changed to protect the people involved.

Editor: Pam Pugh
Interior Design: Ragont Design
Cover Design: Smartt Guys design
Cover Photo: Adam Jeske
Interior Photos: Adam and Christine Jeske

Library of Congress Cataloging-in-Publication Data

Jeske, Christine.
    Into the mud : inspiration for everyday activists : true stories of Africa / Christine Jeske.
        p. cm.
    Includes bibliographical references.
    ISBN 978-0-8024-5879-7
    1. Christianity—Africa—21st century. 2. Africa—Religious life and customs. 3. Africa—Social life and customs. I. Title.
    BR1360.J47 2009
    276'.083—dc22
                                                                        2009031694

We hope you enjoy this book from Moody Publishers. Our goal is to provide high-quality, thought-provoking books and products that connect truth to your real needs and challenges. For more information on other books and products written and produced from a biblical perspective, go to www. moodypublishers.com or write to:

Moody Publishers
820 N. LaSalle Boulevard
Chicago, IL 60610

1 3 5 7 9 10 8 6 4 2

Printed in the United States of America

CONTENTS

NOTICING THINGS ①

"Truth is holy, and truth-telling a noble and useful profession; that the reality around us is created and worth celebrating; that men and women are radically imperfect and radically valuable."[1]

The curtains in my bedroom turn from grey to sunrise peach. Dogs bark, calves bleat for food, and someone is hammering. There's a smell of smoke from a wood fire and the hum of water boiling for my husband's tea. A chill in the air draws me back under the covers.

The woodstove belongs to our neighbors on the left. They are the laborers who clean our landlord's home, drive his tractor, dig postholes, and shovel calf manure. They use sticks to beat the grass for snakes as they walk and eat cornmeal porridge with *shebo* vegetable sauce. They speak Zulu, and while "African" might seem a more politically correct word, in South Africa they generally go by the simple term "black."

Our neighbors on the right are "white," but in every sense they also consider themselves South African. They have a five-foot wide-screen television. The father is known locally as "The DSTV guy." He drives around with his black employee making installations and repairs in five-star hotels and the homes of the wealthy. Their children play cricket and will leave for boarding school when they're thirteen. They have three vehicles plus a four-wheeler, three motorcycles, and a horse. They invite us for *braais* where they roast big slabs of steak on a barbecue fire.

Between them, there's us, with our electric stove, the refrigerator, and our flush toilet. Our children speak just a few words of Zulu. We attend a Zulu church and see Zulu people every day, but on weekends we invite foreigners and whites to our potluck dinners. We drive a four-wheel-drive truck and a motorcycle. We own a lawn mower, a vacuum, two cameras, and two computers worth more than everything in our Zulu neighbors' homes.

This little South African microcosm that I call home is a constant reminder of the way the world works today. There's a strange juxtaposition of my white landlord, his son raising Holstein calves, the Zulu laborers with their bathtub outside for washing clothes, and me with my overseas bank account. It's a world where every choice I make will be viewed by neighbors on every side, and a world where I can make the deliberate choice to stop and notice my own neighbors too.

NOTICING THE STORIES NO ONE TELLS

I planned to move to Africa straight out of college. I imagined a purity of life in eating cornmeal I pounded myself, carrying my own firewood, and reading by candlelight. I attended the University of Wisconsin at Madison, which happened to have an excellent African languages and literature department and a class that had gained some local fame. Harold Scheub, a wiry American with more energy in the classroom than most college students on a Friday night, taught a class called "African Storyteller." The class was often among the first courses on campus to fill to capacity at five hundred students.

I had little intention of diving too deeply into African studies, but hearing rave reviews, I tried to register on a whim.

I got in.

And so began my love of the stories of African people. This professor had carried a tape recorder up and down the African continent recording stories from anybody who talked—grandmothers, traditional healers, chiefs, and children. To me, this was a new way to see Africa—not as a dark continent of cannibals and lions, or as a suffering continent of malnourishment and HIV victims, but as a treasure field of dignified people, brilliant and beloved by God.

I craved more. By the end of college, I had completed majors in English and piano performance but had also squeezed in classes like "Survey of Africa," "Malnourishment and World Hunger," and "Subtropical Agriculture." I started applying for the Peace Corps, but instead I married my husband, Adam, a Spanish major, and we headed to Central America together.

For the next eight years, Adam and I pieced together service opportunities in Nicaragua, China, and the United States. By the time we moved to Africa, I was seven years older and the mother of two preschoolers. As much as I still dreamed of raising my children in a remote village, teaching them to live by candlelight and hand-hauled water, we decided we should start with a country that had English as a major language and a government that didn't march soldiers with automatic weapons down our streets. Finally in 2006 we found a job in South Africa, a country on that continent I had dreamed of for more than a decade. With that first memory of the African storyteller class always in my mind, I expected Africa to drip with culture—grandmothers telling folktales around fires, children singing and dancing to centuries-old music, generations held together by traditions passed along on spoken words.

However these stories were nowhere to be found in the

South Africa I encountered. A South African woman my age told me frankly, "No one ever told me stories, especially not about Africa." A fifteen-year-old didn't know that elephants or impalas ever roamed free in her country. Holding my old copy of *Indaba My Children*, a five-hundred-page collection of traditional South African stories written in 1964, I considered chucking it across the room. Why had people misled me to believe that these stories still meant anything to a people smothered by the forward push of time and Western culture?

The Zulu people I met in South Africa wore T-shirts and jeans. They aspired to have jobs as graphic designers and taxi drivers. They believed a strange mix of secularized ancestor worship, often as distant from its origins as Easter bunnies from the crucifixion. Most difficult of all, I found no local spokespeople for their culture. I met plenty of outsiders talking *about* black people. Even in our job as managers of a microfinance organization, I found myself coming *at* the South African people instead of moving *with* them. For all our well-intentioned efforts to provide a hand up, not a handout, we were joining a world of foreigners trying to solve Africa's problems.

After eighteen months in Africa, I still felt disconnected from the people we had come to serve. One day I resolved to sit for over an hour in silence to consider why we came to Africa. Finally, that afternoon I wrote six words on a scrap of paper in bold letters. It was a Bible verse I had sung since my childhood in Sunday school: "Seek first the kingdom of God." Not "seek a successful project." Not "seek the end of poverty, or HIV, or orphan-headed households." Seek *the kingdom*. So I started looking. I remembered another Bible verse about the kingdom of God: "Blessed are you who are poor, for yours is the kingdom of God" (Luke 6:20). If I wanted to see God's kingdom and His blessings in action, I decided I had better start with the basics and hang out with the poor.

NOTICING THINGS FALLEN APART

What I found when I started seeking, at least on the surface, still included a lot of brokenness, fear, and dirt.

I remembered reading Chinua Achebe's classic African novel *Things Fall Apart* in the first survey of Africa course I took in college. The book introduces as its protagonist a well-respected village man. He is a fighter, a hunter, and the head of a large family. Then a missionary comes to his Nigerian village. The rules of society shake and crumble. The African man loses his identity, his stability, his will to live, and the book ends with his suicide.

I talked about this book with a friend when I visited her in Zambia. We discussed the legacy of colonialism and what hope there is for Africa in the global economy. Now centuries have passed since the trade and colonialism interrupted the delicate balance of local economics and subsistence living. While plenty of people still live in mud-brick homes, their psyche is forever altered by knowing what lurks in the world beyond a television screen. We attended a rural Zambian church and listened to American Christian hits on the radio in this country that proudly calls itself a Christian nation. We talked to young Zambians, and I heard the same dreams I heard among South African youths. They weren't dreaming of owning more cows or raising more peanuts. They wanted to get a job, a computer, and a ticket overseas. Christianity, Western goals, and a global economy have penetrated even the most isolated corners of these African countries, and there's no going back.

All this left my head spinning. What is South Africa, and what are the countries following in its wake, if not beaded garments and pounded grain? Postcolonial realities and globalization are sweeping away traditional Africa, and what will fill the void? My American friends back at home see Africa in the news as a continent of AIDS patients, malnourished babies, and child soldiers. If we follow the stereotypes in the media, the African continent is little more than a desperately failed attempt to imitate the West. Is this Africa's only choice? If there's no going back, is there any way forward? Does it all end in the mass suicide of an entire continent of cultures?

When I began writing this book, things weren't looking hopeful in my corner of Africa. As an American who had lived in KwaZulu-Natal province of South Africa for just under two years, I found the news and gossip of Africa intriguing and un-settling. The national power company had just initiated "load-shedding." Due to major gaps in the power company's budget and planning, the company suddenly announced massive elec-tricity shortages. The solution they chose was unpredictable, sweeping power shutoffs that caused chaos and uproar. Fac-tories sent their employees home early, stoplight outages cre-ated hours of jammed traffic, and people waited stranded in mall elevators. While most developing countries have grown accustomed to unpredictable shortages of electricity, water, and other services, this hit South Africa as a step backward. Conversations everywhere turned to dire predictions for this country that could produce 20 percent of the world's gold and hold 40 percent of the continent's telephones but couldn't manage to provide its people with electricity.

Eventually the electric company phased out the power cuts, but this relief arrived just in time for worldwide sky-rocketing food prices—new fodder for complaint. All this came as a hard blow to a country where the thrill of freedom had worn thin in the fourteen years since the first free elec-tions after apartheid. Black economic empowerment, integra-tion, and a black middle class sounded great in theory, but for the people still jobless in the countryside, it was easier to see the increase in the cost of living than any improvement in quality of life.

Meanwhile South Africa watched Zimbabwe, its neighbor to the north, stumble and collapse. In that country, inflation rates topped 10 million percent.[2] In 2008, yet another election failed to oust President Robert Mugabe from his twenty-eight-year dictatorship. Three million Zimbabweans, a quarter of the country's population, had emigrated by February of 2008. Four thousand immigrants were crossing the border into South Africa every day. As these immigrants crowded into historically tribally charged slum neighborhoods, a wave of xenophobic violence swept South Africa in May of 2008. Zimbabweans and other African immigrants were beaten out of their homes, "necklaced" with burning tires, and trapped by fear wherever they turned.

If one chose to look further, Kenya, usually seen as more stable and developed than some of its neighbors, was spinning in tribal violence. Sudan had been treading genocidal ground for decades, Somalia was in anarchy, and wars festered in the Democratic Republic of the Congo. Few other stories of Africa ever made international news headlines.

As the months passed in South Africa, I watched the near collapse of two different foreign-based nonprofit organizations. I puzzled over the reasons. It was more than the gaps in staff skills or administrative shortcomings. I saw a broader lack of understanding by the overseas donors and visionaries. Too often those writing the newsletters and publicity for their organizations turned to shock-value horror stories, paired with oversimplified solutions. They felt forced to make donors feel like their money made a difference, quickly and quantifiably.

A local South African newspaper asked me to interview residents of a small town, asking their thoughts on South Africa's progress over the last ten years. The answers hit everywhere on the spectrum. One respondent described her view as "very, very negative." Those looking at the physical surface pointed to decayed roads, unofficial segregation in housing patterns, corrupted local governments, and plenty of crime. They were looking for a way out. Not surprisingly, many with the economic means to leave for Europe, Australia, or the United States were taking those opportunities. A countrywide survey showed that in 2007, 39 percent of South Africans said they were seriously considering leaving the country, as opposed to 18 percent in 2000.[3]

Still other residents described the last decade in South Africa as "very, very, *very* positive." One man described changing race relations, saying, "Fifteen years ago it was 'I'm over here and you're over there.'" Another man said, "There's a good spirit here now." And another woman pointed out that while still only "a very small proportion" of both blacks and whites venture into social circles of the opposite race, the world was changing for the better here. "What you've got to get your head around," she said, "is that it's not just blacks or whites, but the whole mix."

What I saw in common among those with positive answers was a Christian perspective. Instead of focusing on the quality of roads and the price of cornmeal, they were looking for internal changes in the hearts around them. Those looking for Jesus amidst this turmoil saw Him, and nothing could dampen the hope they saw in Him. They saw church members breaking down cross-cultural barriers, women who lived in poverty themselves volunteering among their sick neighbors, and teachers working tirelessly to create a better world for young people.

One educated white woman explained that she grew up reading North American Christian books and sermons that are largely available in South Africa. "It was as if we were looking to America for what God was saying to Africa." Then she went to a conference in Zimbabwe that changed her life. As part of a tiny minority of white attendees, she and her husband had their "minds blown away." Pastors from Nigeria, Uganda, Rwanda, and other countries across the continent preached "what God was saying to Africa." The woman returned home and began assisting a Rwandan woman in organizing reconciliation seminars for South Africans of all races. Later, her husband would die of knife wounds inflicted by a burglar. Still she refused to give in to pessimism and began accepting speaking engagements telling her story of forgiveness. When I asked her about crime in South Africa, she said, "Don't talk to me about that. I believe we live in a safe area. I believe South Africa is great, and God is doing great things here."

There were people like her, who saw hope in the Africa that God made. They saw, like my friend in Zambia, that there was no way back. But they were looking for the way forward.

NOTICING THINGS FALLEN—
AND RISING AGAIN

Christians stake their belief system on one God who created every culture and every individual. That God has a view of how each person's specific circumstances—no matter how broken and disjointed—can grow into something beautiful. Christians believe that God entered the world as a human being, right in the middle of a specific time and place that in many ways reminded me of what I saw in South Africa. Jesus was born in a Jewish family under Roman rule. The Jewish people had once been politically and economically strong, but then had suffered years of occupation and oppression. They maintained laws and norms that for many had become no more than routine, and their identity as a people was shaken.

What many of them hoped for from Jesus was a solution to their oppression, a political upheaval to reinstate the independence and greatness of their nation.

Instead God had a different plan. Jesus did not wipe out their problems in a burst of political power, He just entered into the world, sank deep into all its troubles, and took them onto Himself. He touched sick people one by one and they were healed. Often He spoke over them at the same time that their sins were forgiven. He taught them by the tens and by the hundreds and thousands how to be transformed into people who would go on spreading what He was teaching, what He called the "kingdom of God." Along the way He experienced insults, temptations, exhaustion, slander, and beatings. He walked straight through the messiest mud this world could fling at Him, culminating in an unfounded condemnation in religious and political courts and a humiliating and torturous death on a cross.

If all He had done was live a good life and die, though, He would have remained only an admirable figure of Jewish history. The reason His death matters is that it shook something in the spiritual realm that still touches you and me today. He stood face-to-face with the evil of His time, and also with the very heart of evil in all of time. His dying moans voiced God's own unfathomable grief over every individual in history, each of us, for our part in rejecting what God intended for our lives.

And the important thing, the most wonderful thing, is that three days after His friends placed Jesus' dead body in a tomb, He rose to life again. This physical resurrection was more than the rejuvenation of a patient whose heart stopped beating for a few seconds on the operating table. This was the healing of all healings, a pivotal moment in history. By walking on the earth again, alive in His radiant but scarred body, Jesus declared for all time that God brings good out of evil, life out of death. He was not only the best human who ever lived, He was God, entering the mess that human sin makes of the world and addressing the punishment that humans deserve for making that mess, and fixing it all at once. He gives each of us an out, a reprieve from the punishment and the separation from God that we each deserve, if we will give our lives back to Jesus who gave us His life. And when we do that, we are able to join Him in His work.

The trouble is, we don't see it all fixed at once. When people believe and trust in Jesus today, He continues healing and forgiving us, one person at a time. But healing and changing individual lives and then multiplying those individuals to change entire cultures is a slow process. At the same time, evil, suffering, and death continue. Jesus promised that in the end of time He would wipe away every tear and make an end to mourning, pain, and death (Revelation 21:3–4), but the end of the world can seem like a long time to wait.

In the meantime, the word that gives me greatest hope for countries like South Africa (and, really, for all countries) is *sanctification*. I don't mean sanctification in the way it might conjure up pictures of people wearing white robes and hovering around an altar lighting candles. It's a complex word that theologians can spend volumes mulling over. What I mean here is sanctification in the way of being changed into something new, something holy from the inside, something God made to exist in the muck of daily life, to fill that space in a way it has never been filled before.

Just before He died on the cross, Jesus prayed for all those to come who would follow Him. His prayer is recorded in the book of John (17:15–19):

My prayer is not that you would take them out of the world but that you protect them from the evil one. They are not of the world, even as I am not of it. Sanctify them by the truth; your word is truth. As you sent me into the world, I have sent them into the world. For them I sanctify myself, that they too may be truly sanctified.

Jesus planned a legacy of people around the world whom He would sanctify as He makes them capable of following in His footsteps. People who are not taken out of the world, but who are right in the world. People who live inside their culture, but think differently. People who are sanctified through the same power that brought Him back to life.

Jesus was the first new living sprout out of a chopped-down tree stump. And these sprouts are everywhere we turn. Between every stereotype I had ever imagined of South African culture and every reality that grates on my outsider expectations for what this culture could be, there is a present-day reality of what God is making here. I speak for South Africa because that is where I live, but there are more pictures like these in broken places anywhere on earth. When I look for Him, I see Jesus walking all over in this muddy world as surely as people watched His dirty sandals slap across the earth two thousand years ago.

Let me be clear—Africa is an enormous continent, more than three times the size of the United States, with fifty-four countries at the time of this writing and more than a thousand languages. Across the African continent, cultures will vary more than between Canada and the tip of Argentina. I cannot offer details on every country from Swaziland to Libya. The stories in this book are of people I met in the relatively small KwaZulu-Natal province of South Africa. The majority people group here is Zulu, but whites and other minorities struggle through their roles here too. Unemployment is high, people scrape by on welfare grants, and the HIV rate is around 40 percent of the adult population.

I should also warn you that this book has an important difference from most of what you will read about Africa, or development, or nearly any international subject. Journalists are taught from their earliest training that one way to sell stories is to find superlatives—stories you can describe with words like *first*, or like those ending in *-est:* biggest, saddest, sickest, poorest, newest. The stories you are about to read are not chosen because they are the only, the worst, or the best of anything. Most involve average people—the people I happened to get to know. Their lives are similar to many others, but I don't pretend that these individuals deserve to represent others in their "type." None of them think of themselves as spectacular, just as people living the lives they were born into.

I chose this approach intentionally because in real life we do not come to understand a culture by seeing only its best and worst—its superstars and tsunamis. We come to know a culture or an issue one person at a time, one interaction at a time. Each time I tell a story of another African person, my intention is to reveal another piece of the real Africa today. These people were not just subjects to interview or news blips of the day—with few exceptions they are my friends, people I knew for months or years before I began to write. In the few pages devoted to each of them, I have tried to let you know them as individuals, each as unique as every one of your own friends.

Finally, I will warn you that this is not a book of social answers. If you want a political and social analysis spelling out the roots of injustice and telling you what to do tomorrow to help, there are other books to explore. When people ask me what they can do to really make a difference in the developing world, the first recommendation I give is: Watch. Listen.

Meet people. Ask questions. This is a book to make that possible without having to buy a plane ticket (although I hope some of you will do that, too). Studying stories is a learning technique worth practicing. When Jesus spoke in parables, He left people to figure out some of their own meanings and applications. In the same way, this book is intended to spur your mind and heart in a lifelong search for solutions, not just to digest my ideas.

My hope is that reading these African stories will provide a starting point for bridges across the world. I have chosen each story to open a window to broader issues—education, HIV, small business development, evangelism, the roles of foreigners, urbanization, and more. This is not simply a book about development or missions, though; it is a book about mud, and Christ there. There is mud in our lives no matter where we live or work. Rather than just learning about the issues and people in these stories, I ask you to learn from them. Notice how they have relied on God through difficulties, and apply what you learn to your own neighborhood, workplace, church, and family, as well as the rest of the world. Take time to answer the questions at the end of each chapter and, better yet, talk through your ideas with a group of people. Come up with questions of your own and dig until you find answers.

Whether you are taking a business trip to Nigeria, planning a short-term mission project to Brazil, volunteering as an English tutor for immigrants, or just looking for a view outside your daily life, I pray these stories will challenge you to press on seeking and catching glimpses of the kingdom of God.

INTO THE MUD:
SOFI

2

On Easter Sunday at noon, the white families from the churches in the little South African town of Winterton were driving home for family feasts of ham, roasts, and grilled steaks. Meanwhile the families from our Zulu church were swaying to the beat of huge amplifiers at a weekend-long conference. My husband, Adam, had joined our Zulu church for the conference, but I stayed behind with our two children. I planned to gather with a dozen other foreigners at an American couple's home for a home-away-from-home Easter party.

The sun shone from a perfectly blue sky, lighting the line of mountains in the distance and feeling as much like a spring day as one could ask for in South Africa, where the reversed seasons mean Easter comes in late summer. Summer in South Africa means rain, daily downpours of it, and the last few nights had been no exception. Dirt roads could be slick as ice for mile-long stretches. By noon on a sunny day like this, one might hope to barely make it up a steep driveway without slipping into a ditch and needing a four-wheel-drive tow—but it was never a sure thing.

We traveled in a caravan—two American short-term volunteers and I in a tiny car in the lead, our friend Sofi with a cheap SUV full of passengers in the middle, and another friend with a four-wheel-drive truck in the rear. When we turned into Sofi's driveway to pick up salads and appetizers, Sofi opted to stay clear of the already deeply rutted mud driveway. She turned her vehicle to cross a field, through grass as tall as an adult, chugging uphill. Then she met a patch of swamp, invisible among the grass. The wheels spun, mud flew, and she went nowhere.

Out we climbed from all three vehicles—adults, children, and babies of every size and shade. Sofi's adopted son, Hlo, a high-school-aged Zulu young man, stripped off his shoes and leveraged a log under the back wheel to hoist. The Americans and I threw our own shoes in a pile and sloshed in, pushing and heaving as mud splattered our Sunday dresses and suit coats. Ten-year-old twins who were staying with Sofi for a few weeks climbed out and joined the pushing. Sofi's six-year-old mixed-race son, her white two-year-old daughter, and my two preschool children stood on the sidelines cheering and questioning. Soon they were stomping around in bare toes, covering themselves with mud along with the adults.

We backed the four-wheel drive truck in and tied it to the SUV with a rope, but before the SUV moved more than four inches, the four-wheel drive truck was stuck, too. We loaded all the children into the back of the truck and told them to jump up and down in the hopes of weighting the back wheels enough to get a grip through the mud. Pushing and grunting, shouting and laughing, we shoved that truck out. But Sofi's was deeper than ever, past the center of the hubcap.

Sofi flopped down in the wet grass. Another foster child, a six-month-old baby, began whimpering from the car seat where he had sat watching the whole ordeal. Sofi fished in a bag to find a bottle.

I squatted beside Sofi. "We'll find a tractor tomorrow."

She shrugged and grinned. "Happy Easter!"

So off we drove, packed two-deep in the two remaining

vehicles. Sofi's vehicle could sit in its mud for another day. We were late for a pot roast and an afternoon of dancing, singing, and laughing. A little mud wasn't going to keep us from celebrating the resurrection.

I had known Sofi for almost two years, and I knew this Easter celebration was one of many next steps in Sofi's long journey, mostly laden with mud. Sofi was the first foreigner I met who had tasted Africa and swallowed— hook, line, and sinker. Or maybe better said, Africa swallowed her. In Africa, she found the deepest love of her life and experienced the deepest hurts of her life.

She spent her spare hours and money building relationships with her Zulu neighbors and assisting wherever she could.

I first met Sofi through photographs. Adam took a ten-day trip to South Africa to investigate various work and volunteer opportunities six months before the rest of us moved, and among the hundreds of photos he brought home were several of Sofi's family.

Adam summarized the basics of her tragically intriguing story. She grew up moving between England and Australia, then came to South Africa as a young adult. There she fell in love with and married a Zulu man, birthed a son of that marriage, learned that her husband was HIV positive, and nursed her husband until his death.

But she stayed. Her husband's family sent her a high-school-aged boy—now essentially an adopted son—to help around the home. Two years later she found herself pregnant by a Romanian boyfriend who left before the child was born. The child, a blonde little girl, rounded out Sofi's single-mom family with three children ranging everywhere on South

Africa's racial spectrum. Still she stayed, somehow captivated by life in South Africa and what it could be. Through years scraping by in restaurant and farm jobs, Sofi spent her spare hours and money building relationships with her Zulu neighbors and assisting wherever she could. It made for quite a story.

An Australian journalist friend of Sofi's thought so, too, and put the story into print. When it ended up on the front page, donations poured in. Sofi quit her job and plunged into full-time development work.

All this I knew, but still in my mind it read more like a newspaper article than the life of someone who could become one of my closest friends. I knew enough about development work to know this woman's depth of entry into the community was more than that of the average volunteer, and I suspected there was more behind that sinking into a foreign culture than a newspaper article could tell. I stared at the photo of her son Doong, from her mixed marriage. His little dreadlocks spiked out in all directions around a smiling confident face, the color of smooth mud.

Also among the pictures of Sofi's house was a shot of her kitchen. I searched the photo for insight into the life of the woman who lived there. Cups and utensils hung from a bicycle wheel contraption, catching light from a cracked window. Jars of all shapes and colors—filled with lentils, pasta, cornmeal, and spices—rested on plain wooden planks along a mud wall. Sofi's home was a strange hybrid of Zulu and Western building techniques. As was typical for Zulu homes, the kitchen was a mud-walled building separate from the rest of the home.

Six months after I stared at those pictures, my husband, our two children Phoebe and Zeke, aged three and one, and I packed bags and suitcases and flew the twenty-four-hour journey to our new home in South Africa. We moved into a quaint old thatched-roof house at a farm two driveways up the road from Sofi.

As we arrived, our new coworker mentioned that Sofi's kitchen had burned to the ground. Wildfires were common in the South African dry season, and in fact we would beat out two of them in our own yard during the first week we lived in South Africa. Sofi and two visitors had been lucky to survive— they waited in her bathtub while the fire raged past, setting the tank from her gas stove into a tremendous explosion. Sofi had lost a lot of things in Africa.

Before we had so much as learned the uses of the half-dozen skeleton keys for every room of our house, Sofi pulled her beat-up grey pickup into our driveway to greet her new neighbors. She stepped out wearing capri pants with stripes in a half-dozen colors and a distinctively hippie-style shirt. Reaching back to tie back her disheveled blonde hair, she shouted a British-Australian accented "Hellooo!" and popped open the back doors of the truck. While her daughter Maya, just under a year old, made herself at home in the dirt drive-way, her son Doong ran straight into the house to find our children.

We were thrilled to have this new seasoned outsider friend, and plunged into questions. Where could we buy nails? Could we borrow her drill? When could we hear her thoughts on the microfinance project we had come to manage? How could we meet the Zulu neighbors who lived across the road?

Within minutes, Doong plowed out of the house tugging Phoebe by the hand, and a fast friendship began. He was two years older and about six inches taller, but in the coming weeks his name became a common household word. "Doong never wears shoes. Doong's not afraid of stepping on pokey things. Doong can climb that big purple-flower tree. Doong can speak Zulu. Doong's my best friend."

When Doong joined us for lunch one day, he offered to pray before the meal. I had heard from mutual friends that Sofi was not a Christian, so I accepted Doong's offer with curiosity. "Thank You, God, for the birds that sing, and please help everyone who is sick or lonely or afraid." He opened his eyes and tore into a sandwich. Phoebe, whose prayers usually included little more than "thank You for the food and my bed," opened her eyes and stared at her older-brother-hero. For over a year she would repeat the exact words nearly every time she prayed. Obviously someone had taught this boy to pray, and I wasn't about to haggle over who or how if he was teaching my own daughter, too. Sofi's faith remained a mystery to me. She never spoke of it, and I suspected she had wounds that I was better equipped to deal with in prayer than in conversation.

Almost daily, our families crossed paths. Our one-year-old son, Zeke, scooted and wobbled around the farm with Sofi's daughter Maya, who was progressing straight from her first steps to climbing sinks, ladders, and refrigerators. Seeing the perfectly healthy and happy girl regularly caked top to bottom in remnants of cornmeal, tree sap, and red-brown soil had a soothing effect on any remaining concerns for our own children in this wild land.

Even the two dogs that came with our rental home shared their lives with Sofi, freely roaming over fields from her house to ours, sniffing out the best after-dinner scraps, and casually staying a few days at a time at either house. We spent long hours with Sofi, exchanging meals, haircuts, and gardening advice, and we never managed to exhaust our list of questions. But still I knew little of her past besides the rough outline I had heard thirdhand.

One afternoon Sofi invited the kids and me for an afternoon out for tea and scones at a bed-and-breakfast farm. We sat at a table on the lawn of the bed-and-breakfast watching the sun set while our children bounced on a trampoline.

"This is where Robs and I met," Sofi mentioned casually between bites of a scone slathered in layers of butter, jam, and whipped cream.

It was the first time I had heard her mention her husband's name or bring up her past. "He worked here?" I asked.

"He was the farm supervisor. I used to meet him here and we would ride horses all up into those hills." Phoebe was shouting for a push on the swings and Maya and Zeke tugged at the same tricycle. The conversation ended, but on the drive home I imagined Sofi and her Robs riding their horses past five-star tourist resorts and between the eucalyptus plantations, stopping at the Zulu homes scattered along hillsides. As night fell our children grew quiet in the backseat, and we enjoyed uninterrupted conversation.

"They freaked out. They were like, 'What on earth are you doing? You're off in a completely different culture, a different country, in dirt-poor conditions, and we can't be there to help. What are you doing?'"

"These roads are a bugger in the rainy season," she said as we rounded a narrow curve.

I had heard stories of this rainy season—bridges under water, roads impassible for weeks at a time. Soon enough I would learn to maneuver over rivulets, searching out the two highest paths tire-distance apart on any semblance of road. I had arrived in South Africa in the dry season, though, and I still had little reference for these stories.

"Just around here, I think it was." Her pickup strained as

we came over a steep hill where the road was pitted with six-inch ruts. "I was living in the kraal, and Doong was just a baby."

Later I would piece together what else surrounded Sofi in the moment she was describing. She had far more on her shoulders than the average new mom. It had been over a year since she told her family that she had moved in with a black man and had begun planning a wedding. "They freaked out," she would tell me later. "They were like, 'What on earth are you doing? You're off in a completely different culture, a different country, in dirt-poor conditions, and we can't be there to help. What are you doing?'"

Most white South Africans in the area would have agreed if she had taken time to listen. It was only five years since apartheid had ended, and for her to move into a mud home with a black man in the middle of a Zulu tribal area was unheard of.

Later, though, when her parents came to South Africa to meet her husband, they loved him. They stayed for the traditional Zulu wedding ceremony and loved that, too. In their wedding picture, Robs holds a Zulu cowhide shield and wears the clothing of a Zulu warrior or groom—a sparse loin covering and several bands of hide and beads around his chest and arms. Beside him Sofi in her own Zulu clothing grins with an innocent joy.

Like a typical Zulu wife, Sofi moved into the homestead of Robs's extended family, a place they would call home for over a year. One month later, Sofi suspected she was pregnant. She and Robs went together to the health clinic to confirm her pregnancy. Like all pregnant women in South Africa, Sofi took a series of blood tests, including one for HIV. Robs joined her. Her tests came out clear and healthy. Robs was HIV positive. It was a day to celebrate the beginning of one life and to grapple with the impending end of another.

34

Life went on—Doong was born, Sofi and Robs made plans to buy a farm of their own, and Robs showed no signs of sickness. Then on the night Sofi was describing, hidden tensions rose to the surface.

"I came up this road at night in a downpour, just buckets." She downshifted to second as we climbed the hill. "And I got stuck." In the dim twilight I could imagine her here, a newlywed carrying on her shoulders the stress of uncharted life choices, just months from the tragedy that would shake her to the core. "I just stood outside crying—I was totally drenched, the only white lady around, a baby shrieking in the truck, and up to my axles in mud. If I ever hated Africa, that was it, right there in that moment."

From the day they learned Robs was HIV positive, they had begun the process of learning about and fighting this disease. At the time, AIDS was only beginning to gather attention in South Africa. Even finding a place to test his CD4 count took numerous phone calls. Getting antiretroviral treatment could take six months or longer. As a precaution, they had started the process. The first CD4 count test came out high, meaning the virus had progressed very little, and Robs could expect to remain healthy for months or years. They purchased their own farm, and their dreams of offering community development support were just taking root. "It was not a big deal then," she would recall of their naivety.

When Doong was six months old, Sofi returned from a three-day trip and found Robs complaining of a miserable toothache. Robs refused to get treatment, and soon his entire mouth was infected. The infection proved devastating to his compromised immune system. Until then they had been a normal happy family. Robs carried the new baby on tractor rides and horse rides on days when Sofi worked.

All that ended suddenly. "After the infection, he got

shingles. Then he got meningitis. In three months he was barely walking," Sofi recalled. "Then one day he didn't get up. Then he stopped talking." It was only then that this all sunk in. "It was like a revelation. *Oh no, he's going to die.* I had no phone numbers of any of his relatives, nothing. I was totally unprepared, and I couldn't leave the house to find anyone." A week after he stopped talking, Robs silently passed away.

Sofi hardly speaks of that time. When I asked one day what it was like to marry someone with HIV, she said simply, "It sucked."

Eventually she began spending most of her time with people affected by HIV in the township and rural areas nearby. On any given day, she might drive to the hospital with her SUV packed to the limit with sick people, fill out paperwork for an illiterate grandmother's government retirement pension, stand beside orphans or disabled people in lines at government offices, or meet with leaders of hospitals, churches, schools, or social welfare agencies. She washed people who had been left to die in their own waste, worked late into the night with soot-blackened hands evacuating people from wildfires, and delivered a young mother's baby. It became rare to find only Sofi and her own children living at their home. Volunteers began to come and go regularly from around the world, and a family friend came daily to help in Sofi's house and to run a small day care for Zulu children in the area. She also welcomed the occasional abandoned baby, child, or family into her own home.

At first while she was working, Sofi would take Doong to the Zulu women who worked on the farm next door. Doong was born in England, raised in South Africa by Zulu grandmothers, and he has lived suspended between the two worlds ever since. His name proves a puzzle to spell, and a puzzle to pronounce for anyone wanting a logical linguistic explanation.

Sofi and Robs chose Lungelo (pronounced Loong-ay-lo), meaning Privilege, for their son's name. Soon they gave him the nickname Lungi (Loong-ee), then the playful Doong-a-Loong, then just Doong. His name, like his world, is a curious hybrid of English and Zulu and a creative mother in between. Fluent in Zulu and English as soon as he began to speak, tall for his age, and as strong spirited as his mother, Doong spent his preschool days leading a troop of Zulu youngsters around their farmsteads, traipsing barefoot through blackberry bushes and among horses and cows. When Doong started school, Sofi fought a battle every morning to get him to wear shoes.

While Sofi might find herself ill at ease at formal birthday and tea parties with the white families of Winterton—especially when she pulled up with a ragtag load of family and foster friends in all racial shades—Doong was perfectly at home in this crowd, too. At any gathering, he often ended up marching around like a pied piper with a train of admirers.

After those first months we spent living at the farm up the road from Doong, Phoebe met many other children nearer her own age, whom I always expected to become her closest friends. Somehow Doong seemed to maintain his place at the top of her list. After her fifth birthday party with a dozen children, as I tucked her into bed, I asked if she had fun playing with so-and-so, naming a few friends' names. She nodded dreamily until I got to Doong's name. Then she perked up and scowled at me. "*Mom*, of course I did." Her voice had that teenager sass I didn't expect to hear until she was well beyond her five years. "Doong's my best friend. You *know* that."

Three-year-old Zeke chimed in, "Doong's *my* best friend!" An argument ensued until I explained that Doong could be a best friend for both of them—and I suspect for a lot of other people, too.

At age seven, Doong spent a week home from school

recovering from the mumps. He was immunized, but still suffered a week of flu-like symptoms when he was exposed to the disease. "Someday maybe they'll hate me for not paying them more attention," Sofi laughed as we talked about her children. She lived more than axle-deep in poverty, giving so much of her heart and time in the Zulu community that it was never easy to strike a balance as a single mom. Her intention has been to never sacrifice her children for a cause, though. When Doong reached school age, she made the difficult choice not to send him to the low-quality farm school where his Zulu playmates went, but instead to drive into town daily to the higher-fee school where all the whites go, along with Indians and blacks with enough money for transport and fees.

Already from an early age, Doong seemed to understand what she lived for. "He'll say 'that child looks really hungry or sick,' and he's always saying 'why don't we give this away to so-and-so?'" When I asked what hopes she has for her children's futures, she said, "Really just that they know Jesus and follow whatever He wants. At one level I'd hope they stayed in this community and did something to help, but that's just because that's what I do. Whatever it is, if it's following God, that's fine."

What does the Bible have to say when you're lying in bed at night alone with two children hearing thieves rip the solar panels from your roof?

This was not always her perspective. When she explained recently why it was she came to Africa over ten years ago, she said, "I suppose it was God, but I wouldn't have called it that. There were too many implications. I never wanted to be labeled a Christian because I knew too many Christians I didn't want to be associated with. But I was brought up with Catholic values, and I would pray to God. I believed in love, peace, and all that, but it was different." Thus little Doong could teach Phoebe to pray for the poor and sick, but his mother was not about to spend a Sunday morning taking him to church.

Then nine months into my family's time in Africa, something unexpected began to unfold. One Sunday afternoon we stopped by for a visit, and Sofi casually dropped her news of the day. "I went to church." She avoided eye contact, pulling Maya down from a wobbly bench and scooping a rusted bolt from the girl's mouth in one sweep of motion. "I needed to make some friends, and that's where all the nice people make friends, isn't it?" There was sarcasm in her voice but also something beneath the surface, something she carefully protected that hadn't found words yet.

Weeks later, we spent the afternoon at a campground swimming pool, one of several tourist spots whose owners she knew personally and whose facilities we could use for free. At a lull in conversation, I asked Sofi hesitantly, "How was church this week?"

She leaned back on a towel, her eyes hidden behind sunglasses. "Every time I sit in church, I just cry. I don't know what it is. I just cry."

It would be a long time before she would call herself a Christian, but already her heart melted at the idea of a loving God who could relate to suffering people. "I just want to learn," she told us one day. "I need people to talk about this with." Soon, almost all the development workers, foreigners, and misfit Christians we knew were gathering weekly at her house for an unusual sort of Bible study. We took turns choosing subjects or verses, tackling issues that some people who have been Christians all their lives never face. What does the

Bible have to say when you're lying in bed at night alone with two children hearing thieves rip the solar panels from your roof? What about Robs—where is he now? And why are people poor? What does the Bible say about a woman with a mental disability, raped repeatedly, struggling to raise her two children, sterilized without her consent? We talked about forgiveness, economics, church services, judgment, and mostly about the basics of loving God and your neighbor. Sofi's work and her passion for the poor people around her had not changed, but suddenly she had better explanations and the awareness of a higher power, Christ Himself, who walked with her every day.

One Friday morning, Sofi announced she was going to get baptized. She had been meeting with a pastor who explained the core of Christianity to her: that God chose to send His own Son, Jesus, into the world out of love for us; that Jesus died to pay the price for everything we have ever done wrong and will ever do wrong; and that Jesus rose from the dead and promises eternal life to all those who believe in Him.

"It's about submission," she told us. "It's like I said to God, 'Really, really, I'm Yours.' For a long time I was fighting this, like I didn't like what I saw some Christians doing when they weren't in church on Sunday." She looked around the room, as if she was about to apologize but saw understanding faces and went on. "But you guys, you just went on loving me as I was. And I realized this isn't about what other people are doing anyway. It's about forgiving and being forgiven, and it's about God. And now," she sucked in a shaky breath and reached for a tissue, "there's such a relief in doing everything for God, and having the strength that comes from that."

For Christians, baptism is the ceremony that publically seals the deal. Immersion in water symbolizes the washing of past, present, and future wrongs, as well as the wetness of a new birth into a spiritual life. Sofi turned to me. "Can you ask your landlord to use the river?"

The morning of the baptism, I walked along the riverbank that bordered our landlord's pecan farm. The water was high, with rainy season weather dumping another inch or more of rain down the banks every night. The churning water picked up sediment, making a lively flow of muddy liquid, with no bottom in sight. The farm was named for a ten-foot waterfall, Mpofana Falls, just above the stretch where she planned to enter the river. Often I would sit on our porch at night beneath a wide stretch of stars, listening to the waterfall's ceaseless pounding.

I had lived by this river for nearly a year but still couldn't quite shake the stern warning from the local doctor's wife: "I wouldn't doubt there are crocodiles in that river." It wasn't unrealistic. Sofi once mentioned casually after a party she had attended how she finally met "the woman whose husband was killed by a crocodile." South Africa is no stranger to dangers lurking in the water—hippos, crocodiles, and snakes.

When Zulu children drowned mysteriously, people often blamed snakes. One woman told me with tears in her eyes how her nine-year-old daughter "went down" in a river one afternoon as if she was held by something, and "it must have been a snake—a very big snake." By the time other children went for help, it was too late—neighbors dragged the girl from the river but never found the snake. Most white people deny the existence of such large human-squeezing snakes, but for most Zulu people they exist in a different form of reality, in a blurred area between symbolism and realism. I have heard stories told by reliable, educated people about snakes vomited from the mouths of repentant sinners, snakes underwater training traditional healers, and a snake like a rainbow arching from a woman's body at her baptism.

As I continued along the water's edge, I remembered a day some weeks after we moved onto this property. Sofi's family visited, and we walked along the river to a large flat rock where the children could shape mountains and rivers in the sand. The afternoon summer sun was blazing, and soon Doong stripped to his underwear, begging to swim. Sofi waved him on, and in he went. In minutes, our own children followed. I cringed at every step and ripple, imagining those slippery rocks, those snakes, and those crocodiles.

But Sofi knew about these. And still, here she was to get baptized. The Assembly of God church Sofi attended practiced full immersion, and that meant two options: the Winterton Country Club swimming pool, or this river. For Sofi, the choice was clear—not the country club, a traditionally whites only, white-owned, pay-to-enter club, where many of her dearest friends would hardly be welcomed. Instead, the river. A swift-flowing, dirt-brown flow, carrying debris over hidden stumbling blocks. There was nothing safe or clean about this river.

I liked to think that the Jordan River where Jesus was baptized was muddy, too. Jesus did not fear the dirt caked between His toes and was not ashamed to scrub the dirt from between the toes of His dearest friends. He touched forbidden unclean leprous fingers and spoke to men and women of the wrong class, the wrong nationality, and the wrong religious practices. He smeared mud and spit onto blind eyes to heal them. Somehow right here in the dirt of life, not in any purified or filtered holy water, plunging into whatever dangers, hurts, and sorrows life holds, Jesus would come. I could think of no better place to experience the true meaning of baptism.

In they went that afternoon—Sofi and her pastor arm in arm—inching along, wading ever deeper, around rocks, trying not to stumble on the invisible bottom. Finally they stopped at a spot just as deep as their hearts. The pounding waterfall drowned out the words of the pastor's prayer, but from the shore we could see that long before her face touched the water, Sofi's cheeks were wet with tears. Storm clouds rumbled behind us. In half an hour rain would pour over all of us. Raindrops would sizzle on the grill of roasting meat, and we would unfold picnic baskets of salads and pies on the damp grass. The children would take their turn splashing in the brown water. I would wrap my arms around Sofi's dripping shoulders to exchange a long teary hug. We would celebrate this eternal story that weaves into many of the stories of this book and my own story as well. With a bowed head and a release, into the mud she went.

QUESTIONS *for discussion and reflection:*

1. What does the metaphor of entering "into the mud" mean to you?
2. What challenging choices have Sofi and her family faced in living literally and figuratively around a lot of "mud"?
3. If you were raised in a middle- or higher-income home and chose to serve among people in poverty, what difficulties would you expect to face? How would you handle these challenges?
4. Name examples of people in the Bible or people you know who lived and worked amidst the difficulties of human life. How did they handle these difficulties?
5. Read Philippians 2:5–9:

   Your attitude should be the same as that of Christ Jesus: Who, being in very nature God, did not consider equality with God something to be grasped, but made himself nothing, taking the very nature of a servant, being made in

43

human likeness. And being found in appearance as a man, he humbled himself and became obedient to death—even death on a cross! Therefore God exalted him to the highest place . . .

How does the writer, the apostle Paul, paint the example Jesus sets for His followers? When you have faced difficulties in your own life or in the lives of people around you, how has your own attitude compared to the attitude of Jesus Christ described here?

WHERE ARE THE MOTHERS?: THEMBI

3

I met Thembi (pronounced "Tem-bee") the first Sunday after we arrived in Africa. Our family had decided to attend a Zulu church that conveniently translated much of the service into English. It happened to be Mother's Day, and halfway through the service the pastor made an announcement in Zulu that I could only understand had something to do with mothers. Then from the back of the room, an old woman's raspy voice began a repetitive, swinging, hand-clapping song that brought the whole congregation to their feet. As we sang, all the mothers began dancing their way to the front of the church —stooped grandmothers, young women with babies strapped to their backs, women of all ages, grooving in a circle.

Among them, one woman of about my age caught my eye. Her hips swayed beneath a black dress as her legs bowed and bent to the music. A wooden necklace bounced on her throat, and her long swaying braids framed the calm smile on her face. There was something about her confidence that held my gaze. I made up my mind to introduce myself to her after the service.

Later I would learn the words to the song. "Where are the mothers who love the Lord?" sang the congregation. Twisting, swinging, slapping her feet into the cement floor, this woman lifted her deep alto voice among the others as they replied,

"Here are the mothers who love the Lord. Here we are!" I would also discover that this woman in black was neither married nor technically a mother, but the more I understood of her life, the more that image of dancing on Mother's Day seemed her perfect introduction.

After church the entire congregation filed out in a chain so that every person could shake hands with every other person. When I made eye contact with the woman from the dance, I greeted her in my new fumbling Zulu.

"Nice to meet you, sister!" She ignored my Zulu and plunged into an English conversation. "My name is Thembi. Where you come from?" She clasped one of my hands and drew our arms around each other's waists.

I was hungry for friendship, and within a five-minute conversation, I invited her to visit our home the following Sunday. She accepted.

Thus began a story that would remind me more of Cinderella with every passing sentence.

The next week, as we sat in my kitchen eating grilled cheese sandwiches and sliced cucumbers, Thembi offered to teach me to make *ijeqe*, a Zulu steamed bread. We laughed over my awkward attempts to pronounce the word, which includes a click of the tongue on the letter "q." I had no other plans for the day, so we stirred up the flour, sugar, salt, water, and yeast, and then sat together under a blanket in the living room to wait for the dough to rise.

We sat facing each other, legs side by side on the couch, making small talk for a few minutes. Then Thembi said abruptly, "I need to tell you my story."

I scooted down under the blanket a few inches, rested my

head against the couch, and smiled. "I would love to hear it."

"I had two brothers and nine sisters." Thembi spoke each word with care. She placed one hand neatly in the palm of the other and held it over her heart. "I was the last one. When I was thirteen days old, my father died. So my mother went to work in Johannesburg, and she sent me to live with my aunt."

Thus began a story that would remind me more of Cinderella with every passing sentence. While Thembi's ten siblings lived together under the care of the eldest sister, the infant Thembi lived with an aunt who was every bit the evil stepmother of the fairy tale. Instead of two cruel stepsisters, Thembi lived with a half-dozen older cousins. They modeled their mother's attitude that Thembi was an unwanted burden in an already overstretched household. The aunt forced Thembi to call her "Mom," but as soon as Thembi was old enough to work, Thembi became essentially the slave of the family. Often she would sleep outside on the ground, afraid to go inside and face her irrationally ruthless caregiver.

For the first fifteen years of Thembi's life, she had no idea what her real mother looked like, nor did she know that her mother sent letters and money that her aunt confiscated. Instead, her life was about survival. She was thin as a wisp, often bruised, and desperately meticulous out of a gnawing fear of punishment.

As the story unfolded, I couldn't help wondering what would happen to this Cinderella character. Would she meet a prince? What would keep her from giving up on wishing, becoming jaded with the world's suffering, and turning into a bitter old hag? Was there any hope that her own scars might shape a heart sensitive to the suffering around her?

One evening when Thembi was in high school, she walked home, washed her school uniform, and finished as many chores as on any other night. At nightfall, she lay down on her bed, exhausted, and leaned over to blow out the candle. Suddenly she heard scuffling under the bed. A hand reached out to touch her arm, her leg. Someone was climbing on top of her. Survival reflexes snapped into place. Thembi fought with every ounce of her tiny frame. "Help! Rape!" She screamed at the top of her lungs, but the louder she screamed, the louder her aunt in the next room turned up the radio. Later Thembi surmised that her aunt had accepted money from a corrupt *sangoma*, or traditional healer, giving him permission to rape Thembi.

I said, "Why did you help save my life? I want to die!"

"I don't know how I fought him off," Thembi recalled, shaking her head and pausing for a deep swallow. "I know God protected me."

Screaming, kicking, fighting tooth and nail, Thembi tore herself free and plunged out the door. She collapsed in a field and laid her head on a torn and bloodied sleeve for a fitful night of sleep.

It was not the first time she had slept outside, but she decided it would be the last. The next morning she walked to school, still wearing her stained clothing.

I leaned forward on the couch with my fingers squeezing the blanket.

"I was being like crazy." Thembi shook her head and her long braids swished around her face as she described the day. "My teachers saw me and said, 'Why do you look different today?' I was a good student, you know. And I had no uniform on and was bloody. I start to cry."

Thembi walked out of the school and down the street to a local shop. She bought a small package and brought it back to the school, then opened it and ate—rat poison. Her classmates found her unconscious in the school courtyard, and the principal rushed her to the hospital.

I found myself wishing this might be the point in the story where Cinderella could open her eyes and find her fairy godmother, wand in hand, ready to dress Cinderella in a magical gown and slippers and send her off to the man of her dreams in a glimmering palace.

Instead Thembi opened her eyes in the hospital to see her mother—not the "stepmother," not the fairy godmother, but her own birth mother. Unlike in Cinderella's story, Thembi's mother had not died, she had only moved to Johannesburg. In Thembi's heart, though, she was as good as dead. When the elderly woman beside Thembi's bed introduced herself as Thembi's mother, Thembi was not in a mood to make this a happy reunion scene. She was furious. "I was being very angry with her. My mother was crying. She was very confused and very sad."

Thembi stayed in the hospital for several weeks. "At first I had oxygen tubes in my mouth, but I wanted to shout at everyone. I said, 'Why did you help save my life? I want to die!' But they counseled me."

There was no fairy godmother and no prince for Thembi. Instead, she credited God for freeing her. Thembi's mother returned to work, but social welfare workers found a new home for Thembi with a neighbor of her aunt, a Christian woman who took her to a church that surrounded her with love and counsel. In time, Thembi began to let go of her anger at God, her mother, her aunt, and the world. As she grieved for wrongs committed against her, she saw that God also grieved. Eventually she entrusted God with her future, her wishes, and her whole life. Having found peace with Christ, she discovered Him giving her a new attitude of peace toward her family. Slowly, loving relationships grew between Thembi and her mother and siblings.

When she finished high school, she knew she needed to find a way to support herself, so she moved to the large city of Durban, even though she knew no one there. On the day she arrived in Durban, she wandered down a city street, carrying only the few coins she owned. She knew it was a hope beyond reason that led her there, searching for some place to stay, for some way to earn money, or some miracle to happen, but she was determined to trust God in any situation. As she stood at a bus stop, a stranger struck up a conversation with her. Thembi refers to her as a "sister," meaning a black woman and a Christian. The woman asked her what she was doing in Durban. Then she invited Thembi to her home. By the end of the day, the woman insisted that Thembi stay, cleaning her home in exchange for room, board, and small wages. Thembi stayed for more than a year. The woman, like a true older sister, counseled Thembi as she processed her bitter childhood. She taught Thembi how to save money, and she encouraged Thembi to find opportunities for a better future. Eventually Thembi found herself working in a construction company office and saving enough money to build herself a small home.

"It was a healing time," Thembi said. She was well on her way to a Cinderella ending. If not a castle and a prince, at least she had the best that most rural Zulu people ask for—a good job in a city and a home of her own.

At this point Thembi reminded me that our dough must be risen, and it was time to set

As she stared into the baby's round eyes, she saw herself there. Had anyone cradled her like this? Had anyone sung to her?

the dough in a double-boiler pan to steam on the stove. It might have been the end of a happy story, but Thembi had more to tell. As we settled back into our place on the couch, she began describing the next chapter of her life.

One morning when she was working, Thembi received a phone call from a relative. One of Thembi's older sisters had died, leaving four children behind. By now Thembi was visiting her mother and older siblings regularly, slowly healing the relationships she had missed in her childhood. This death came as a heavy blow. Thembi went home to her mother's house and paid for her sister's funeral.

As the visitors returned home, Thembi found herself in her mother's home, holding in her arms the youngest orphan nephew, still just a baby. As she stared into his round eyes, she saw herself there. Had anyone cradled her like this? Had anyone sung to her? Was this baby destined to experience the same abandonment and fear that marked her childhood?

When Thembi went home to Durban, she carried with her this youngest orphan boy. She resolved to give the child the best she could. As a single working woman barely out of high school, she felt ill equipped to care for the baby. She hired a woman to care for him during the day and then later brought him back to her mother's home where the baby's other three orphaned siblings lived. Thembi sent money regularly to pay for a caregiver to help her mother.

Then another sister died. "And another one die. And another one die. And another one die." As Thembi repeated the words, tears pooled in her eyes. She stopped when her voice gave out.

Thembi returned home for each sister's death and paid most of the cost of the funerals. By 2005, all but one of her ten siblings had died. At the time, no one in her rural area was speaking of HIV.

"I don't know why they died," Thembi said. "Maybe it was HIV. They had runny stomachs, and rashes, and sores. So I think so, but I don't know because we didn't test anyone."

Finally only one sister remained. This last sister had four children. "The last one was born of [the] mother's rape," Thembi explained. The sister's husband had committed suicide just a year before the rape. "After she was raped," Thembi said of her sister, "she was disturbed in the head. She hated everything in this world. She left the oldest sons caring for the cows. They ate food from the rubbish can. They slept outside. They did not go to school."

Thembi and her mother resisted their suspicion that the woman was losing her mind. "It was difficult to understand. She was clean. She spoke positive things. She was not like the other crazy people you meet. But she dug a hole in the middle of her house. I don't know why. And she would start building a room and not finish it. And other things. Maybe because she didn't get any help when she was being raped."

Then one day while Thembi was visiting her mother, to their amazement, two boys strolled onto their property. The oldest was fifteen years old, the younger only ten. When they reached the house, Thembi suddenly recognized them as her sister's boys, exhausted and caked in dust.

"I cried tears when I saw them," Thembi said. "From the house of my sister to the house of my mother, it was a forty-five minute taxi ride. And they walked. One boy's foot was swollen. They had no shoes. It was amazing. I looked at them, and you could see, they had big heads and big stomachs. You could see the bones in them. I just wanted to give them all my food. I kept saying, 'Take this food. Take this food. Take this food.'"

The boys never returned to their mother's home. They stayed with Thembi's mother and the growing crowd of orphans. Thembi went to fetch the boys' two younger sisters, bringing the total to nine nieces and nephews at her mother's home. One year later, Thembi's last sister came to stay at the home, too. By now her condition was more than a subtle mental disturbance. She refused food and medicine, and she barely spoke. Finally on February 9, 2005, she passed away, the last of Thembi's ten siblings.

Until then, Thembi had tried to be strong. She had held her job, sent money for the children and her mother, and paid for funeral after funeral. Now something snapped. She could carry no more. "After the funeral, I was just sobbing and sobbing. We didn't have any money left. Nothing. We couldn't even pay for the funeral, not even a mortuary. We just wrapped her in a blanket to bury her." Thembi did not return to work. She stayed at her mother's home, crying and crying. "I was like crazy. None of my friends wanted to talk to me because I was just crying."

Without her knowing it, one of those friends, a woman from Thembi's church, took a bold step on Thembi's behalf. She approached a white man who had recently bought a large plot of land in the area. His vision was to build a rural home for orphans. Just fourteen days after the funeral, this man arrived at Thembi's house, followed by two more cars filled with American volunteers.

Thembi began to giggle as she explained the scene. Nearly two dozen Americans climbed out of the cars, snapping pictures, touching the frightened children, roaming everywhere. "I was cooking butternut and mealies (cornmeal porridge)," Thembi said. "I was so embarrassed to open the pot. That was all the food we had, and I didn't want them to see it."

Piecing together a conversation with her limited English and the white visitors' limited Zulu, Thembi came to understand that the Americans had come offering to take Thembi's family to the orphanage. The foreigners would return in two days to fetch them if they agreed.

That was when Thembi made the bravest decision I can imagine. Knowing just a few words of English, she packed up the six youngest children, climbed into the van with the foreigners, and moved into the orphanage as her nieces' and nephews' caregiver. There she learned to speak English fluently and grew to love welcoming the foreign volunteers who come to stay at the orphanage. She also became the caretaker for another three children who also call her "Mom."

People in the prime of life all around them—teachers, nurses, shopkeepers, mothers, and fathers—silently passed away.

"And that's where I live. That's my story." Thembi opened her hands palms up and shrugged. By now the bread was steaming in a pot on my stove, and a warm smell filled the room. I clasped Thembi's hands in mine and we sat in silence for a long moment.

In the coming months, I began visiting Thembi every Wednesday for a lesson in speaking Zulu. Later we spent several mornings a month together working with a beaded craft organization. One weekend she invited me to visit her mother's home, and I met for the first time the grinning woman I already knew well from Thembi's story. Thembi and I came bearing a sack full of grocery store fried chicken, so as not to burden her mother, but the tireless old woman insisted on killing and cooking her own chicken for us anyway.

The orphanage lay in an epicenter of HIV and a crisis of deaths. Estimates placed the HIV rate in the 30 km radius at around 40 percent of the adult population. That made it about the highest HIV rate in South Africa and among the highest in the world, but by no means the only place in the world experiencing the terrible crush of HIV. On the surface, you might not have noticed it. The orphan village housed only a few dozen children, and it was a last resort for most of these children. If they had grandmothers, aunts, or neighbors who could provide for them and keep them safe from abuse or neglect, they would stay with family. Volunteers in the community, called home-based caregivers, often stepped in to care for their sick and dying neighbors and help orphans find social services or nonprofit help. For many of these caregivers, their lives were not easy either. They faced difficult choices. They gave food from their own tables. Meanwhile people in the prime of life all around them—teachers, nurses, shopkeepers, mothers, and fathers—silently passed away. The community was stretched to its limits.

While the orphanage almost literally saved her life, Thembi hoped to move into a home of her own. Through volunteers at the orphanage, she collected donations to build a six-room house for herself and the twelve she now considered her children.

As I wrote this, the walls were built, the doors and windows are in, and only the roof was lacking. The move would not be easy. She and her aging mother would be hard-pressed to earn money and care for the children. Thembi had nearly completed a local computer course, and she was earning some income through a Zulu beaded crafts organization, but even with some welfare money, it would be a stretch to feed the large family. Even if she could leave the children while she found work, her home was in a rural area where job opportunities are few.

As a rare thirty-year-old woman without a boyfriend or children of her own, Thembi learned to rely heavily on prayer

57

and faith in God. Her story had no prince and no fairy god-mother, but one good God is shaping a happy ending not only for Thembi but also for the second generation of Cinderella children that she cares for. "I keep trusting God, and I don't give up," she told me. "I open my Bible, and I sing. And I like to pray *very loud*," she laughed. "And God is very faithful. I know what He did for me."

QUESTIONS *for discussion and reflection:*

1. How was this friendship important to the author as an outsider to the culture?
2. What factors caused children in this story to lose or be separated from their mothers?
3. Why was it a difficult choice for Thembi and her family to move to the orphanage?
4. What additional support could Thembi use if her family moves into their own home?
5. Read and reflect on Psalm 68:4–6:

Sing to God, sing praise to his name, extol him who rides on the clouds—his name is the Lord—and rejoice before him. A father to the fatherless, a defender of widows, is God in his holy dwelling. God sets the lonely in families, he leads forth the prisoners with singing; but the rebellious live in a sun-scorched land.

What hope does this description of God offer in the global HIV/AIDS crisis?

IN THIS TOGETHER: PHOEBE

4

On a fall Sunday evening, we sat with Sofi sipping drinks and watching the sun fade behind the mountains behind one of our favorite restaurants. Our youngsters shouted happily as they raced around a grassy yard and climbed a fence about a meter tall.

Suddenly we heard Zeke crying. Doong shouted, "Zeke's head is stuck!" Sure enough, our little boy, who had always had a notoriously large head for his age, was stuck with his head at a 45-degree angle between bars of the fence. Realizing no one was hurt, Adam cracked a joke as I went to free him.

At that moment Phoebe, who was hanging facedown with her stomach resting on the top bar of the fence, looked down at her crying brother. She seemed to reach out to help, tipped forward past the balancing point, and crashed headfirst to the ground. The full weight of her body landed on one wrist twisted beneath her head. I ran the last steps to help.

Zeke had already freed himself when I arrived, but now Phoebe was holding her arm and shrieking. She had never had a high tolerance for pain, so when she whimpered through our restaurant meal, we shushed her and encouraged her to lie down on a restaurant couch and rest. It wasn't until that night, during the second, third, and sixth time that we went into her room to calm her sobbing and wipe away the tears dripping into her hair that we knew this was serious.

There were two hospitals relatively near our home. Emmaus Hospital, just a fifteen-minute drive from our house, offered free and reduced rates for nearly anyone, so it was usually packed with the poorest of Zulu people. The other hospital, in Ladysmith forty-five minutes away, had charged us an arm and a leg when we went there to get the chest X-rays required for our visas. Those high fees kept it less busy and also paid for more doctors and specialists, making it the unofficial upper-class hospital.

I believed that often the first step of loving a neighbor was choosing to dwell in their neighborhood— eat what they ate, shop where they shopped . . .

I weighed the options. This wasn't a life-threatening condition. I generally disliked the idea of driving and paying for privileged facilities when I could join my Zulu brothers and sisters in what was often their only option. I believed that often the first step of loving a neighbor was choosing to dwell in their neighborhood—eat what they ate, shop where they shopped, travel how they traveled, and today, to wait for health care where they waited. Besides, how bad could it be? If all else failed, I could always take her to Ladysmith afterward.

At eight fifteen in the morning, Phoebe and I stepped out of our car into a maze of small buildings labeled with more Zulu signs than English. Emmaus Hospital was built nearly a century ago as a mission and seemed to have added buildings haphazardly ever since. I found a sign for "X-ray" and pushed Phoebe up a steep hill, thankful that Adam had suggested we bring the stroller.

At the top of the hill, four buildings faced one another in a square. Examining their signs, I chose the one listing X-ray, along with a half-dozen other treatments. A woman sat at a desk outside.

"Papers." She said it simply.

"Papers?" I asked.

"Where's your papers?"

I didn't know.

In broken English, she informed me that I must first register at another building, back down the hill. I gripped the handles of the stroller tightly to keep from dumping Phoebe face-first out of the stroller as we bounced down the steep hill of uneven cobblestones back to where we had entered the hospital compound, to a building labeled "Registration." A line stretched far out the door.

Again I weighed my options—was it worth the wait, when I could just drive to another city? Was the line moving? Were all those people in the room inside waiting for what I would wait for? I watched a woman just ten people ahead of me take her turn at the window. Good, we were moving. Surely it wouldn't be long once we could register.

I stared at the shoes of the girl in front of us. It seemed they had once been white, but now were brown and caked with half an inch of mud on the bottom. It had rained all last night. I pictured her waking up before dawn that morning, suffering from some illness or enduring the complaints of someone else in her family, sliding through mud, perhaps down a long muddy road to catch a bus. Here I was, already pushing my limits of patience, when I had merely climbed out of a warm bed, eaten a healthy breakfast, and driven my own car fifteen minutes to get here. If I thought I was here to demonstrate some kind of solidarity with these people, I had a long way to go.

As I lifted the stroller over the step into the registration building, Phoebe's arm jostled against the stroller. She let out a yelp, and was still crying when my turn came at the registration desk. The receptionist, unbothered by the crying, rattled on about what to do with the half-dozen papers she was sliding toward me. I tilted my head as close as possible to the hole in the pane of glass between us and pleaded with Phoebe to hush. I misunderstood the woman's instructions. I was supposed to get Phoebe weighed by a nurse in that building and return to the registration desk, but instead I pushed the stroller up the hill a second time to the X-ray building, got rejected, and rolled back down to registration again.

Back in the registration building, I spun in circles trying to make head or tail of a roomful of stone-faced patients. Were they waiting for a nurse to call their name? Was there some order to their seating? Finally I ducked my head into the back hallway where the nurses circulated and asked if this was where they weighed my daughter. The nurse scowled, then told me to sit on one of the packed benches lining the hallway. The women next to me did not move to make space for us, and I felt dozens of pairs of eyes staring at us, the only whites in the room, with our stroller blocking half the hallway.

What had just happened? Had the nurse, out of some sort of sympathy or embarrassment for me, just told me to cut in line in front of the fifty or more others on benches in the waiting room next door? I tried to summon the courage to ask. An old woman shuffled past, leaning on a cane, and I tucked my backpack of books, markers, and snacks farther under the stroller. I told myself I couldn't take their preferential treatment; I would rather wait like everyone else. Instead I ran my fingers through Phoebe's tangled hair. I fixed my eyes on the tears drying on her face, and I couldn't convince myself to move.

A few short minutes later, a nurse ushered us into a room and stood Phoebe on a scale, asked us what was wrong, made some marks on one of the several cards in our envelope, and sent us out. On my way out, I spotted the girl in the muddy shoes, still waiting.

I swallowed excuses and guilt shuffling in my mind. My daughter wasn't used to waiting—surely these people were better at it than we were. I knew my internal argument was incomplete, but with my packet of cards and papers in hand, I took a deep breath, leaned my body into the stroller, and whispered a thankful prayer that we were headed for the X-ray room for the third and—I hoped—final time.

What's this? No—it couldn't be! The line had only just then begun to move.

The nurse at the X-ray building directed us inside to a chair and explained that we would go after the woman in front of us. The X-ray waiting room had about thirty people in rows of chairs in front of us, with three empty rows of chairs behind us. I took out my cell phone, hoping to give Adam an update on our progress, but realized there was no cell reception. I turned to the nearest nurse and asked if this was a normal occurrence.

"You must go outside up by the big tree," she said.

I slung Phoebe onto my hip and climbed the stairs farther up the hill to a large pine tree stretching its limbs over the restroom building. Sure enough, my cell phone showed one bar, just barely enough to place the call. The spot was not the highest in the area, or in any other way recognizable as the only place on the property to make a call. I marveled at the insanity of it, and at the mercy of the nurse who told me. It was ten o'clock, two hours after we left home. Feeling optimistic,

I told Adam we were through the worst and should see a doctor in thirty minutes.

For the next hour, we read the couple of books we had packed for Phoebe, and she drew a cat. She whined some, even cried some, but we hung in there.

To my surprise, Sofi appeared suddenly, the only white face I had seen all day. She asked how we were doing, but I steered conversation away from ourselves to keep from letting out the tears that were bubbling just beneath the surface. Sofi talked freely, explaining she was there with three orphans getting a physician's signature in order to register for welfare grants. For children like these, with no birth certificates and no parents, it was a process so complicated these kids would never complete it without Sofi's persistence. The grant money could make the difference between sickness and health, hunger and food, death and life.

As we sat, Sofi pointed down the hallway that she had visited many times before with people in similar situations to these orphans. "There's only one doctor on duty today," she said.

"So what are all those rooms for?" I had watched people in uniforms roaming in and out of the five or six rooms along the hallway all morning.

"They're short staff, as usual," she said. "Those rooms have no doctors, just a bunch of nurses picking their noses." As usual, Sofi offered a dose of humor, cynicism, and straight-faced persistence. She excused herself to track down the official she needed to visit, and I managed a smile in parting.

So we waited. Phoebe smiled and greeted the women near us. One woman a few seats away from us stood and went into a room along the hallway. We must be getting close.

Then suddenly everyone stood up and shifted one seat over. What's this? No—it couldn't be! The line had only just then *begun* to move. The woman next to me must have read my surprise. As I sat in my new chair stretching to see over the seats in front of me, she silently gestured toward a man on a gurney being wheeled into the room. These emergency patients interrupting the line were so far the only people entering those rooms. This was an emergency room as well as a waiting room. The woman shrugged, and I slumped back into my seat and exchanged a half smile with her. Inside I was shaking with anger.

By now Phoebe had hit her limits. She had slept no longer than three hours at a time the night before, and neither had I. Suddenly, at a painful twist of her wrist, she burst into a tantrum and flailed in my arms, kicking the man with the toothache next to me.

I carried her outside and stood listening to her wailing, ready to cry myself. If someone had offered me a place at the front of the line now, I would have taken it in an instant. No one was offering, though. Finally Phoebe's sobs slowed to little gasps and sniffles. I tucked her head against my shoulder and returned to my seat. A nurse arrived with a cup of pain reliever, and I couldn't have been more grateful. Phoebe gulped down the medicine.

We shared the raisins, peanuts, two peaches, and one of the two granola bars I had packed. It was nearing one o'clock, five hours after we left home. I had not planned to need lunch.

Sofi stopped in again, just finished with the orphans' meeting with a doctor in another building. "Their birthdays were printed wrong on their birth certificates." She was rushing the words, sucking on her lip between sentences to fight back tears. "We waited six months for those certificates, got this stinking far, and Home Affairs faffed 'em up." All they could do was restart the whole process, nearly a year of work. For the orphans, their long outing today was only one in a long string of lines, waits, and social services far overstretched.

As Sofi took the children's hands to leave, she turned and stared into the distance above our heads. "It's like, this would be a good time for God to show up." At that point, Sofi was beginning to call herself a believer, but these words were the story of her life that constantly pressed her faith to its very limit.

The doctor left for a lunch break, and patients lined up out the door while we waited—nobody moving, a room filled with the silent sick, for another hour.

Meanwhile Phoebe, drugged on painkiller, was flying high. She wandered in circles between the patients, singing to herself. I stared at the man in front of me. Blood dripped down his arm from a red bandage onto his ragged jeans. A nurse draped a sheet over his lap, and he took his turn with the doctor. I spoke in Zulu with the woman next to me, learning that she had a four-year-old boy.

"You know what song that was?" Phoebe interrupted us as she climbed onto my lap. I confessed I hadn't been listening to her babbled song.

"It's called, 'The Lord Is Here.'"

Phoebe had heard a lot of Christian songs in her three years. But this was no real song I had ever heard. This she made up, just today. I watched her slide back off my lap and continue her rounds through the rows of chairs, quietly singing, "The Lord is here, the Lord is here now."

On a bench across from us, a boy about seven years old sat with his arm in a sling. He quietly watched Phoebe. After a while, Phoebe noticed him and paused her song to give him the same curious investigation, but neither spoke.

The line moved on, and we sat just three people from the end. Phoebe sat on my lap, I read her a story for the third time, and in a few minutes her tired body slept in my arms. I tucked her gently into her stroller and leaned forward to rest my head on a handle of the stroller. The doctor left for a lunch break, and patients lined up out the door while we waited—nobody moving, a room filled with the silent sick, for another hour.

At two o'clock the air inside was stuffy and hot, and I went to stand outside. My eyes wandered to a large mural formed of earthy brown cement or clay on the side of the X-ray building. The mural showed a man holding the limp body of another man. The ribs of the limp man showed as ridges in the wall, and he tilted his head back, either sick or dead. The man holding him seemed to study his face with compassion and grief. Both men wore simple draped cloth. Knowing it was a mission hospital, I supposed it was something biblical, but I realized there was no clear signal of who the men were. The Good Samaritan helping a bloody traveler? Or was the supporting man Jesus, holding a sick person He was about to heal? Or was Jesus the limp man, dead in the arms of a friend? As I puzzled over the picture, I found it ever more intriguing. There was no way to know whether either man was Jesus— the one dying, or one holding the dying.

Back inside, I watched Phoebe's head bobbing left, then right. In my mind I saw Jesus two thousand years ago, like my daughter, lying helpless at the mercy of God's power in this place full of imperfection, on the way to a life full of every kind of human suffering. I heard the voice of the doctor back from lunch calling in the next patient, and realized that Jesus had faced desperate crowds of sick people just like that doctor. Jesus had also felt the weariness that the next patient felt as she rose to her feet and hobbled into the room. He had comforted others, like the teenage girl across from me whose shoulders supported her mother from the side. I imagined Jesus in the car with the three orphans and Sofi, who was probably already on the phone to set a date to visit the same offices again. And when a man with a foot-long patch of blackened burn on his arm took an emergency turn with the doctor, moving us back another place, I recognized Jesus as the source of my own new reserves of patience.

I shared my last peanuts and raisins with my neighbor, then leaned back and let my eyes rest on each person, one by one around the room as I prayed for them. "Jesus, You know this child. . . . You have felt this woman's pain. . . . Let that man know You are here." My eyes stopped at the boy with the sling. He was probably about a year older than Phoebe. I stared at the small hole torn in his T-shirt, the dirt on his jeans. He cradled one hand around his hurt arm and rested his head on his mother's elbow. A nurse announced it was his turn with the doctor.

At two thirty our turn came. I roused Phoebe from her nap and she silently held my hand into the X-ray room. The young X-ray technician quickly struck up a relaxed conversation that had us both smiling. "If you hold really still," she told Phoebe, "you can have a lolly."

Phoebe did. She moved not a single muscle. Under that big machine, she seemed so trusting, so small. I watched my tired daughter with awe. She took her sucker from the technician and proudly announced that she would eat it only after we were finished with the doctor. Ten minutes later the doctor gave the prognoses—a simple fracture. A nurse wrapped Phoebe's arm in plaster. We unwrapped the sucker. She lifted her arm to put it in her mouth. Suddenly she realized she couldn't move her arm. She panicked.

She screamed at the top of her lungs and did not stop. I tried to listen to the doctor's final instructions, but all I could think of was what every other person in the waiting room was thinking. All those Zulu children waited so quietly and angelically. "White people never wait in lines." I had heard it before, and here I was proving it true. "How embarrassing," I could almost hear them tsking. "That white lady . . . " I was the only one, the only example they had to see today, and I desperately wanted to set a good example of my race.

I grabbed Phoebe's good wrist and dragged her out the door. Still hysterical, her hand opened. As if in slow motion, I watched the sucker soar through the air, hit the tile floor, and shatter in a thousand pieces down the hall of the hospital. Now her screams hit a new pitch, impossibly terrible. I scooped Phoebe into my arms and set her outside the building and left her there while I returned to ask the X-ray woman if she please had another sucker. She

It would not be the first time I would face a question of whether to expose our family to risk and discomfort or to plunge ahead trying to share the lives of the people we came to serve.

did not. I plowed the stroller over feet on my way out, desperate to escape. Phoebe cried all the way to the car. "I hate my cast! I don't like it! I don't like it!" She stared at her arm as if it belonged to an alien monster.

Before starting the car, I paused for a moment to check that I had not forgotten anything in my hurried exit. In that instant, Phoebe looked outside. "Look! That boy has a cast too!" she said between teary breaths.

The boy could not have heard her through the window, but he suddenly turned to her with a huge reassuring smile. She closed her mouth. I watched her wet eyes staring out the window and could almost hear her little brain spinning.

The children locked eye contact and slightly raised their casts toward each other, as if to say: *Look, we are the same. We are going through this together, and they are taking good care of us both.*

From that moment on, Phoebe did not complain again about her cast. We went home and replaced the doctor's yellowish sponge sling with a bright blue bandana. She ate a sucker we found in our cupboard and then slept. When we went back to the hospital in six weeks to have the cast removed, I found the hospital just as overcrowded. That time I gave up after five hours and opted to go home and cut off the cast myself with gardening sheers.

It would not be the first time I would face a question of whether to protect our family from risk and discomfort or to plunge ahead trying to share the lives of the people we came to serve. These were questions with no clear answer. Where would our children attend school? What toys would we buy? What kind of vehicle would we drive? Would I live in a neighborhood known for armed robbery and murders? How long would I give up being able to drop off my children for an afternoon at their grandparents' home?

And whatever I chose, would it make any real difference? Did spending a day as the only white people in a hospital full of people I would never meet again make any difference? If it did make a difference, it was not something we could measure —the day would yield no count of people coming to faith or hungry people fed or churches built. And yet I knew there was value in being there, a value that had nothing to do with the cash we saved.

It is one thing to visit poor people with donations or advice, or visit a sick person with a get-well card and a potted flower. It is another thing to stay and walk with them, to be willing to show our own needs and brokenness, and to take on a piece of their sorrows and troubles. We will never fully know what another human being goes through. Just as we cannot—and need not—try on the pain of a friend facing chemotherapy or depression, we will never know what it feels like to grow up in Haiti or Malawi. If we come from the developed world, we will always have the advantages of a good education, a network of employed friends and relatives, the freedom to walk into a church, and a lifetime of role models. But unless we make an attempt to imagine—even going as far trying to experience—what life is like for someone else with fewer advantages in life, we are missing a beautiful piece of how God loves people.

God gave up His own Son's nobility rights and security in order to love a world full of broken people. Jesus never fought for His own rights, but instead trusted God minute by minute in storms, at sinners' homes, and on the cross. As a way of explaining what it means to be both humble and trusting, He challenged people to become like children. Whether or not Phoebe knew it, her hospital visit for me became a picture of what it means to live and walk into broken situations trusting Christ. It means losing the ability to control our own safety. It means not getting to have every comfort we want. It means getting pushed to the limits of our strength and seeing our emotions spill out in sometimes ugly ways.

And it also means knowing that we need help, and crying out for that help. It means being willing to be in both roles of the picture on the mission hospital wall—not just the one holding, but also the one held. It means letting go of our naïve illusions of our own benevolence and facing our own great need for grace. It means exchanging smiles with people of other cultures and economic levels and knowing we need to receive a smile as much as they do. It is coming to that place of surrender—when the cell phone dies and the bloody-armed man needs your place in line and you realize your own incompetence to meet the needs of even the people you most love—it is there that we meet the God of the poor.

And in knowing Him, we learn to offer His love to others because we are no different—we are going through this together and God is taking good care of us all. We become available, like a child, to dance among suffering people singing, "The Lord is here, the Lord is here now."

QUESTIONS *for discussion and reflection:*

1. List who was affected by the author's choice to go to Emmaus Hospital. Do you think it affected them for better or for worse?
2. Do you think the author made the right choice in taking her daughter to Emmaus Hospital? Where would you draw the line between protecting the safety of your loved ones and showing solidarity with someone with fewer advantages in life?
3. When have you been pushed to your limits of physical or emotional endurance? What did the experience teach you about God?
4. List possibilities of what the picture on the Emmaus Hospital wall depicted. How does the Bible portray Jesus as fitting various roles in this picture?
5. How do those differing roles of Jesus comfort you? How do they challenge you?

OPEN FOR BUSINESS:
NIKIWE

Rumbling over winding dirt roads on my motorcycle, I caught new smells at every bend in the road, carrying the range of emotions of life in a developing country. At one dwelling came the homey smell of cornmeal *phuthu* cooking on a wood fire. At the next came the suffocating burnt-plastic smell of burning trash. Chickens raced past on their skinny legs, flapping frantically for cover in the two-meter tall grass as I caught up with them. Goats scurried away at the first sound of my engine, and cows lazily strolled out of the way. As I picked out the smoothest path along the edge of the road, grass slapped against my helmet.

About every twenty meters, the grass opened to reveal a gate made from sticks strung together with barbed wire that looped over a fence pole on either side. The homes were about as close together as in a North American suburb, but the quality of roads, the tall grass, and the roaming livestock made it hard to think of this as a city.

The white Afrikaner settlers had named the place Loskop, translated "crazy in the head." Not surprisingly, most inhabitants preferred the Zulu name, Amangwe. Called a tribal area, the region was in many places as densely populated as in a city, but the lifestyles were decidedly rural. Land was distributed by a tribal system of asking permission from the chief instead buying and holding official ownership of the land.

Winding along the seemingly random maze of dirt roads, I was always amazed by what I did see as much as by what I didn't see. For a population center of some 200,000 people, Amangwe was surprisingly void of commercial activity. The only visible businesses were a smattering of "tuck shops" selling grocery staples and cold drinks, plus the "shebeens" or neighborhood bars. Earlier in the day I had stopped at the crossroads in the center of town at the area's one tiny bank, next door to the municipal office and a few central shops, but there was no grocery store, no rows of market stalls.

Today I had one last stop to make before home. Last Sunday, a church member had quietly told me that someone in the church, a woman named Nikiwe, might need some help with her business. Nikiwe and her nineteen-year-old daughter often led singing at our church. The daughter had graduated from high school the previous year, and I remembered the conversation when she told me she hoped to attend college. Now the start of the school year had come and gone, and she was still at home helping her mother. I did not have a cell phone number to reach Nikiwe, but I decided to squeeze in a visit on my way home even if I half hoped she would not be at home and I could ride home early for the day.

My husband had insisted on buying our little 200 cc on/off-road motorcycle soon after we arrived in South Africa. At first I was skeptical of the danger, maintenance costs, and prestige of becoming a two-vehicle family, but it took only one ride on a dirt road before I was hooked. Any time I knew I would not need to carry passengers, I took the motorcycle for our regular twenty-minute commute from home to this tribal area. Women in Zulu culture did not usually ride bicycles, much less this dangerous beast of a machine, so I always met a mix of shock and laughter when people saw my female head pop out from under the helmet.

As the cloud of dust behind me grew, I marveled that I could maneuver through nearly any terrain. This was a great improvement over the little car owned by the microfinance organization for which my husband and I were serving as project directors—I had changed three flat car tires in one month. Slowing to avoid a line of women and children filling water buckets at a well, I lifted a hand to wave, then gripped the handle again as I puzzled out the best path between bumps and mud. All this made visiting loan clients almost fun.

Microfinance organizations operate by offering small loans—as small as ten dollars—to people interested in starting or strengthening small businesses.

Almost, that is. Lately I had come to dread most of my meetings with loan clients.

My husband and I came to South Africa believing we could give families like Nikiwe's the push they needed to move a step further out of poverty. We saw improving the living conditions of people in poverty as a strategic role in the overall goal of building God's kingdom in the continent of Africa.

I had always seen South Africa as having a unique importance for the continent. When I first studied African history and culture in university, I wrote in a notebook one day, "If it were not for South Africa, would anyone have any hope left for this continent?" In every statistic, every indicator of development, South Africa shone while others fell further and further behind. In 1994, South Africa's racist apartheid regime ended as black South Africans proudly stood all day in lines to vote for the first time. Under their new black president, former prisoner Nelson Mandela, a radical Truth and Reconciliation Commission offered forgiveness to anyone who confessed to crimes committed under the racist regime, and hope overflowed for this new "Rainbow Nation." If South Africa could succeed, many people reasoned, maybe the rest of Africa could, too.

Then in graduate school, I had a similar sense that in the midst of a world of failing attempts at development, one thing was succeeding. This time instead of a country, it was a method: microfinance. In developing countries around the world, microfinance organizations operated by offering small loans—as small as ten dollars—to people interested in starting or strengthening small businesses. Clients paid back the loans with relatively low interest and the amount they could borrow increased each time they successfully paid back a loan.

Often the programs focused especially on empowering female borrowers, who were statistically more likely to use their profits for food, education, clothing, and other purchases that benefited their entire families. By expecting people to generate their own business ideas and create their own profits, the programs created employment and avoided the "handout" mentality of many development programs. Microfinance was all the buzz in international development. The United Nations declared 2005 the International Year of Microcredit, and in 2006, the year we arrived in South Africa, Mohammed Yunus and the microfinance organization that he founded in Bangladesh, the Grameen Bank, won the Nobel Peace Prize. Microfinance seemed effective, sustainable, and empowering all in one.

So when, on my husband's ten-day trip to South Africa to check out work possibilities, he heard about a brand new microfinance project looking for a managing director, we jumped at the chance. It seemed like the perfect intersection of a promising place plus a promising program. What could be more heartening? In a country of hope, here was a program of hope that used our MBA training. Our assignment was to join the one-year-old project as local directors of a five-year pilot aimed at empowering people in an impoverished rural area to start and improve small businesses. We would experiment until the kinks were worked out of the program, constantly adapting and revising the program until, presumably after five years, we had a model worth multiplying across the country or even the continent.

But it was not turning out to be as easy as we had hoped.

Rolling past house after house, I marveled over the apparent void of entrepreneurship. In every other developing country Adam and I had visited, from Latin America to Asia, we had seen people at equal or lower economic levels churning out micro businesses. Where among these rows of thatched-roof houses were the street vendors walking the streets with bananas and baked goods on their heads, calling out their wares? Where were the noisy lines of market stalls full of spices and smells? How did these people survive, when by all appearances no one was buying or selling anything except on monthly pension day?

One piece of the puzzle was South African history. Under apartheid, black people were essentially forbidden to own formal businesses, so for generations this culture had been void of role models in business, while white-owned businesses gained market share and experience.

Slowing to a stop on my way to my meeting, I peered carefully both ways before pulling out onto the paved road. Across the road loomed the only major employer in Amangwe, a shoe factory. Like many factories across South Africa, it was intentionally placed in a "blacks only" area during apartheid to give

81

black people just enough income to stay alive and out of white areas. These days, other less-developed countries could pay even smaller amounts of money for labor than South Africa does, and factories like these cut their employees to a fraction of what they once employed. The shoe factory still assembled some shoes, but mainly distributed shoes made in China.

Still I believed that the concept of small businesses in South Africa was not a hopeless cause. Some large microfinance institutions in South Africa boasted as many as 35,000 rural clients each, and numerous smaller faith-based programs also offered loans or business counseling that changed lives, one client at a time. I just didn't see many signs of success in Amangwe.

Just past the shoe factory, I passed a familiar house painted an eye-catching sky blue. I was glad today's meeting was not at that blue house.

> *I knocked on doors to hear scurrying, doors clicking locked, and silence.*

It had been one year since I first met the people who lived there. When I first met them, a woman of about my age earned a slim income for the family by selling sausages. As often as she could manage the thirty-minute minibus ride to the nearest city, she would buy a cooler-full of sausages from the butcher, then alert her neighbors and sell until these were gone. Her profits were decent, but her business depended on the sparse finances of her neighbors.

Many families in the area supported themselves almost entirely on the government welfare (called pensions and grants) that gave monthly payouts of about twenty to fifty dollars to retirees, children, and orphans. Families often spent this money within hours of receiving the check and then lived on credit for the rest of the month. A businesswoman like the one in the blue house faced a choice: she could either sell on credit and forever chase down delinquent debtors, or she could compete with the hundreds of other sellers who sprang into action just once a month on "pension day."

As with many microfinance organizations, we used a group model. This meant that a group of five loan clients met together in this blue home. Some were mothers and grand-mothers who sewed school uniforms and the traditional Zulu pinafore dresses, others raised chickens or offered catering services for weddings and funerals. We had carefully trained and tested the group to make sure each member knew and trusted the others. If one member struggled to pay back their loan, every other member would support them with advice and finances. Until every member paid back, no one in the group would be eligible for future loans. Ideally, other groups forming in the area would meet with them to form a club, giv-ing an added level of support. By using a group to guarantee the loan, we could give loans to poor people who could not prove their land ownership or meet other collateral require-ments for bank credit.

This group had passed their training with succinct and correct answers, so we went ahead with their loan. Still I sensed something wrong. They never laughed and never asked me personal questions or gave me the kind of hugs, hand-shakes, and home invitations that many Zulu people offered freely. I never learned the names of the several children star-ing at me from the front porch and peeking their heads into our meetings.

As project directors of this microfinance organization, my husband and I filled precarious roles, arriving as white faces representing money. People saw me as an ambassador of the many white people who had taken so much already from these rural black people. Unless I managed to build relational bridges to clients, the program was better off without me. Here this bridge somehow wasn't reaching.

By the first loan repayment meeting, attendance had slipped to three of the five members. One week no one from outside the home came to the meeting. The following week a grandmother opened the door and explained that the business-owning woman had found work in Johannesburg. She had left the previous day. This meant the grandmother would raise the children and they would see their mother only every few weeks, but it also meant a steady income, presumably to share with family members left behind. Still, for me this was more disheartening than kneeling along a roadside changing our car's third flat tire—I could see that our microfinance project had not been the vehicle of development that fit this family's needs. The old woman shrugged silently when we asked about repaying the loan.

Eventually the woman in the blue house did repay most of her loan money, but having lost their most literate and motivated leader, the rest of the club dissolved. I knocked on doors to hear scurrying, doors clicking locked, and silence. Word came that one middle-aged woman in the group was sick, and soon she passed away, leaving behind only her teenage daughter. The girl struggled to stay in school, but the family's small business died, and we stopped by to offer condolences and say that their debt was canceled.

As I turned the corner past the blue house, I imagined myself back inside, trying to make conversation with a woman I never understood, full of the misperceptions of a foreigner, operating under a well-intentioned vision that was caught in the same web of factors that keep poor people poor. Our list of defaulted loans was growing, and I was wary of adding any more.

As I thought about the meeting I was about to have with

Nikiwe, I imagined myself burying my face in my hands and saying, "Sorry, I can't help your business. All I really know to do is pray."

> *She rattled off the prices and amounts of every ingredient by memory.*

I had been to Nikiwe's house once before, and that time I had come to pray. Nikiwe had called a meeting for church members on behalf of her elderly father and sick sister. I remembered stopping by on my way home from work that day, parking my motorcycle and following Nikiwe and four other church members into a dark room where two people lay on mattresses on the floor. One was obviously Nikiwe's father, but from the shrunken thin face of the woman, she seemed more like a grandmother than a sister. As we prayed, they did not lift their heads or speak, just stared at us from the darkness. In the next six months, both the sick relatives passed away. Now besides her own four children, I expected to find Nikiwe caring for her sister's orphaned two-year-old son.

I turned again at the main intersection in Amangwe where a half-dozen minibuses[4] lined up along the road. Besides shoe factory employees, just about anyone from Amangwe who earned money rode a minibus taxi out of the area. A thirty-minute minibus ride away, a medium-sized well-paved city offered chain grocery stores, factories, and a myriad of businesses owned mostly by people of European or Indian descent. Only teachers and a few civil employees from cities nearby drove into Amangwe to work. This tribal area was a send-off spot, a place people dreamed of leaving, not entering. It was one of the most fled-from and depressed spots in the country, and, not surprisingly, a breeding ground for HIV.

Already the sun was almost as low as the tallest mountains, and I wanted to be home preparing dinner. I rolled up the accelerator of my motorcycle as I climbed a hill, passing the school where our church met each Sunday, then searched for a spot to cut across from the paved road onto the dirt walking path without tumbling into the ditch between the road and the path. I spotted a shallow spot in the ditch, dipped down and then up again into a tramped down path of dirt, brushing my elbows against tall grass along the path. In a minute I popped out into a yard swept clean of leaves and grass.

As I lowered the kickstand and pulled off my helmet, Nikiwe appeared wearing a light flowery apron and gave me a hug. Trailed by her little nephew wobbling along in a T-shirt down to his knees, she led me into a bright room inside one of the four small buildings in her homestead. Stacks of flour bags and cooking oil jugs lined one wall. I sat on a bed, while Nikiwe sat on an overturned bucket. Then the nineteen-year-old daughter pulled in a wooden chair from another room, gave it to her mother, and took the seat on the bucket.

We spent the next hour assessing how much profit she earned in her business and what could increase her profits. Every day, Nikiwe rose long before the sun and started frying *amagwenya*, South African treats resembling softball-sized, lightly sweetened doughnuts. By seven thirty she pushed a wheelbarrow carrying two large buckets full of them to a nearby school.

She rattled off the prices and amounts of every ingredient by memory, and when she paused her daughter jumped in. Both of them knew the business inside and out. At that time they were taking a bus thirty miles to a city at least three times a week. In the course of a week, Nikiwe purchased 150 pounds of flour, ten liters of cooking oil, plus yeast, sliced meat, and other toppings for the *amagwenya*. Her profit was only about five to ten dollars a day. When I asked them what they thought would improve their business, they had answers immediately.

The first idea was that if she could compile enough money to buy a huge amount of stock at a time and pay for a bus seat to stack the supplies, she could cut her transport costs dramatically. We also had a long talk about the importance of sticking to a savings plan to buy an electric stove and to get her daughter into college in one year.

The only problem was that our organization only approved loans for groups. Nikiwe and her daughter racked their brains for anyone in the area who might form a loan group, but Nikiwe finally explained to me her belief that groups would not work in her culture.

Most public South African schools did not provide or sell food for students, so it was common for entrepreneurs like Nikiwe to sell snacks before and after school at the school gates. Four or five other women sold snacks at the same school as Nikiwe, but she dismissed the idea of partnering with any of them. "Those people are not Christians," she said. "Some worship ancestors. Life as a Christian is not the same as the people who are not saved. How can I explain?"

"Since I was a Christian . . . I remember to have hope for tomorrow," Nikiwe said.

Usually when I asked people how we could improve our microfinance organization, they shrugged or gave short indirect answers. Here was a woman with a real theory about why people defaulted on loans, and she was looking for a way to describe it.

"Let me say this," she continued. "These people have never seen a white person really poor. They have never seen anyone who is white who is walking with his own feet, or having no

car, or no home. They think if you are white, you have everything. If I say let's borrow from a white person, they will not
pay back. I know a woman who sells with me, she told us one
day, like boasting, that she did this."

I leaned forward from the edge of the bed. This was what
my husband and I suspected, hashed through in every spare
conversation. There were deep-rooted cultural and spiritual
issues involved.

"Even for black people who lend money," she went on,
"they struggle to get it back. If a person is not saved, I cannot
trust them to pay back."

She explained that she watched many businesses come
and go, while she kept hers going day after day. "Since I was a
Christian, I see that my life is continuing, and I remember to
have hope for tomorrow. Before I was saved, I was like other
people who take the money from their business and when
trouble comes they use it all up, so their business just ends."

I nodded slowly. I had certainly seen that happen. Once
when my coworker left for two weeks during a school holiday,
a dozen young loan recipients she had trained ate their entire
stock of snacks that they were supposed to sell at school.

"Now I know," Nikiwe said, "that I must take my money
from selling, count what I have, and put some in a bank and
use some to buy more stock. So even if hard times come, my
business must continue."

In the coming days, I devised an individual loan plan
specifically for Nikiwe. She started with a ten-dollar loan and
met me one week later to pay back the loan with a tiny
amount of interest. I kept the interest for the microfinance
project, but I then handed her back the same loan money plus
more as her next loan. The rule was that each time she met
me at the bank at our arranged time with her repayment
money, she could take a higher amount. She could choose the

amount of time she kept it, so if she was working up to a higher amount, she could repay weekly, but if she needed the money longer, she could keep it for a month or two and pay it back incrementally. If she arrived late or missed an appointment, she took out less the next time.

It was a perfect plan for her. She knew her business needs well, and never asked for more than she needed because she knew she had to stay in good standing with us—and before the Lord. "I believe God is looking at me whatever I do," she told me one week. "So I have to pay back money. And I want the money to go back to you so it can go to other people."

I had spent so many months learning not to trust anyone making promises that I found it hard to believe Nikiwe, even when she proved herself faithful week after week. She had worked up to a loan of over a hundred dollars paid over a few months, when one week I crossed paths with her at a mutual friend's home. She took my hands and said quietly, "You know. I have been thinking about this, and I don't feel right before the Lord about something."

We sat down on a couch together.

"I am thinking about how money lending works," she said. "In this place, if I want to take a loan from someone, they will say 'You can have fifty rand, but when you pay it back the next month, pay back seventy five.'" I had verified similar outrageous interest rates charged by local loan sharks as well as "payday loan" businesses in the city. For people without proof of land rights or other collateral for a bank loan, this was their only credit option. Our organization charged 1 percent of the loan per week, a simple method that people quickly recognized as lower than the going rate.

"I don't feel right about it. I have money for three months, and you still charge me so little every month. You need the interest money so you can drive your car and give money to other people. I need to do what I feel is right before the Lord."

That month we had arranged for her to make a deposit directly into my bank account instead of meeting at the bank. When I read my bank statement the next week, I realized she had paid twice the interest she was required to pay. I sat at my desk staring at the paper, then laid my face in my hands and thanked God for this woman who broke every distrustful stereotype I had built in the previous year.

A few months later, my husband and I decided to transition from offering only microfinance into providing other services we saw needed among the people of Amangwe. Now I was riding my motorcycle along dirt roads on the way to teach computer classes, offer goal-setting and leadership workshops for young people, teach English in a primary school, and mentor a bookkeeper for a beading cooperative. Still, every month or two I met Nikiwe at the Amangwe bank or at her home as our relationship became more friendship than business.

Like most children, mine loved *amagwenya*. One day as Phoebe bit into a hot greasy one from town, she asked how to make them. I smiled.

"You know who can make *amagwenya*, Phoebe?" I asked. "Nikiwe."

Phoebe remembered the cheerful singer from church, and asked, "Can she teach us?"

So we called Nikiwe. The next day we left the home at 6:15 a.m. and spent an hour in Nikiwe's kitchen. She cooked in a round hut with a fire on the ground and two low benches while the youngest children in the family sat on the floor warming themselves at the edges of the fire. Thick smoke filled the room from the roof down to the height of two small windows. I watched streams of smoke trickling out the windows, and learned quickly to stay on my bench or crouch to keep the smoke out of my eyes and nose.

An opened sack of flour, a plastic bucket of dough, and another bucket of cooked *amagwenya* surrounded Nikiwe. She reached her hand into the dough, rolled a sticky wet ball of dough against the side of the bucket, and slid it into the enormous pot of bubbling oil, again and again in a motion perfected through practice.

"How is your savings account?" I asked.

"It is growing." She paused, then added, "My daughter has registered for university for next year." She kept her eyes on the pot of bubbling oil, but I saw the hint of a smile as the firelight shone on her cheeks.

"You know," she said, "I remember that when I became a Christian, I was taught that in the life of a person, there will be good and bad times. In bad times, I don't move from this position to this position." With her limited English, "position" was the best word she could find, but I got the idea. She would persevere in the tasks and places the Lord had made for her: running a business, improving her family and community, and having faith in Jesus Christ. "In bad times, the Lord gives me strength to stand." I thought of my own doubts about microfinance over the past year and how thankful I was that I had stayed to search out other ways God would use our family in this place.

She shifted a log farther into the fire to control the heat, then dipped a spoon into the pot to roll the *amagwenya* balls. Their brown fried sides bobbed to the surface while the opposite sides cooked.

"Last year was very difficult for me," she said. "When I used to care for my sister—" Suddenly she stopped midsentence. "You know she had AIDS." She glanced up to check my expression. I had guessed the cause of her sister's sickness, but we had never discussed this, and in fact I hardly ever heard the word AIDS spoken aloud in Amangwe. To tell me this took trust and courage.

She told me that some of her neighbors refused to buy her food because they believed it was contaminated by HIV. "I used to pray to God that their minds will be dim and this will not arise in their minds. And you know, my *amagwenya* were so nice, and they were finished before any of the other sellers."

"You and God certainly do make nice *amagwenya*." I smiled. Phoebe was licking the grease off her fingers from her first one, and I was thinking about biting into my second.

"Even now," she said, "the other people selling foods at the school ask me, 'Why does your business always do so well? You always sell so much.' I say it is because of faithfulness— my faithfulness in the Lord."

Oil drips sizzled into the pot as she lifted another strainer full of finished *amagwenya*. As the first rays of sunlight lit the steam and smoke swirling through the hut, Nikiwe spooned out the *amagwenya*, one by one until she had filled her buckets to the brim.

QUESTIONS *for discussion and reflection:*

1. In Romans 12:2, Paul urges Christians, "Do not conform any longer to the pattern of this world, but be transformed by the renewing of your mind." How does Nikiwe demonstrate that her mind and actions are conformed to God rather than the patterns of the world around her?

2. What other examples have you seen of God leading people to break wrong patterns and norms in your own or other cultures?

3. Do you think helping people financially and materially leads to, complements, or conflicts with spreading the gospel? In what ways?

4. What should be the role of Christians in economic development work?
5. How is it possible to make observations about the tendencies of groups of people without falling into judgmental stereotypes?
6. Looking at your own life, what can you learn from Nikiwe's comment about perseverance? She said, "In the life of a person, there will be good and bad times. In bad times, I don't move from this position to this position. In those times, the Lord gives me strength to stand."

THE GOOD SOIL:
MADONDO

"Why isn't Jesus giving you food?"

It was the question every neighbor was asking Madondo. It was 1996, and within a month of becoming one of the first Christians in his village, Madondo had lost his job. He and his wife found themselves with no money, no food.

"Not even a match," he told me as we sat in the cool shade behind his mud-walled home, his thin legs stretched in front of him in the blue work pants common among rural Zulu people. He held back laughter even as he spoke of their desperation.

"My wife was crying to me all the time." He threw his hands in the air. "Finally I broke down and told her 'My wife, stop crying to me! Cry to Jesus.'" Even with his stick thin frame and narrow shoulders, he could make himself heard. "I told her, 'You say we have run out of food and money. I say we have run out of faith.'" (I loved how he always addressed her in customary Zulu fashion as "my wife," and in fact I never heard her first name.)

Following his orders, she carefully cleaned the house. She set their dishes on the table and cleared the ground for a fire, knowing they had no wood to burn. And then she laid her head on the table and cried.

Meanwhile, Madondo took action. He visited a neighbor, asked for food, and received only a handful of cornmeal.

Walking home, his mind knew he still did not even have a scrap of firewood to cook on, but his heart trusted that God had more yet to provide.

Turning the corner to his yard, he saw a rare sight—a car. Out stepped a Zulu pastor from a nearby village. "The Holy Spirit asked me to check on this family," he told Madondo. "And from now on, every month I want to give you money for food."

In Madondo's words, "That day Jesus turned the tables. After this we never went hungry. And this helps everyone here, because I give to others too."

As Madondo talked, the two dogs sprawled on the ground lifted their heads, stretched, and rose to attention. A young woman stood at the gate asking to buy a prepaid airtime voucher for her cell phone from the small shop inside Madondo's home. While I waited for him to return, my eyes rested on the bucket, the water kettle, and the rake along the wall. A fence surrounded a plot of potatoes to my left, rows of corn stretched to my right, and a field of beans grew on the opposite side of the house.

Not surprisingly, the world's poor are migrating to cities in search of work.

I first met Madondo when a friend working in agricultural research invited me to an agricultural demonstration for neighboring village farmers to see and copy the improvements in Madondo's village. In my university and grad school courses on economic development and world hunger, I had often wished I had farming skills or technology that I could somehow share with people in rural poverty. In Africa 80 percent of the people living in extreme poverty live in rural areas, but the majority of their governments' spending goes to urban dwellers.[5] When I came to South Africa, I realized it was surprisingly rare to find a Zulu village so committed to agriculture as Madondo's village, much less new appropriate technology like subterranean groundwater collecting tanks and organic no-till farming. Zulu culture traditionally revolved around raising cattle for food, clothing, investment, and a key element in many spiritual ceremonies. As South Africa modernized, much of the importance of cattle had disintegrated and little came to fill the void.

I had seen graphs comparing historical prices of agricultural goods versus manufactured goods. The graph of agricultural goods takes sharp ups and downs, meaning even when a farmer has a bumper harvest, he or she can never predict whether he may receive barely enough to cover the cost of his seeds or fertilizer. Also over the years, the price paid for agricultural goods has fallen lower and lower compared to the price of manufactured goods. That means the people doing arguably the hardest work—hoeing rows of beans and corn in hot tropical sun—earn less for their work than, well, nearly anyone in the world, and they pay more and more for the spoons, cooking oil, and radios they buy with their shrinking profits.

Not surprisingly, the world's poor are migrating to cities in search of work. The number of people in the world living in cities tripled between 1960 and 2002. In 2007 half the world's population lived in cities, and by 2030 this percentage is expected to reach two-thirds. In the long run, population shift from rural to urban is both a result and a driving force of development as a country shifts from agricultural to manufacturing jobs. In the short run, what many migrants find in cities is rarely the rags to riches stories they hope for. Instead they join the masses of unemployed and underemployed slum dwellers. In sub-Saharan Africa in 2001, 72 percent of city dwellers lived in slums.[6] Others returned home to the countryside disillusioned.

I had come to talk to Madondo because I was curious to hear what became of those left behind in villages. Among the few programs focusing on improving their productivity and well-being, what was working? Who, with education and skills suited specifically for rural needs, was brave, stupid, or self-sacrificing enough to turn down the lure of the city and go back to a village to try to help?

I approached Madondo's story as a case study about working to improve subsistence agriculture. To Madondo, though, the actual growing of food was only a small piece of a larger calling. Not only was he growing corn, vegetables, and beans out of his enriched farmland, he was converting lives marked by hardship into soil for growth.

Before I could open my notebook of prepared questions on farming techniques, Madondo leaned back in his plastic chair and plunged into his life story. Behind him, a goat wound its jaw in circles as it chewed. My scribbled notes grew like a laundry list of all the dirt Madondo had seen in his thirty-eight years. When he was a toddler, his parents divorced and sent him to live with his grandmother. At age fifteen he dropped out of school and went to Durban, a city of 2.5 million people. His parents had never registered him for a birth certificate or ID, and without these he could not legally be employed in South Africa. For two years he did little more than scrape by to survive on the streets of Durban's townships. When it seemed life could not get any worse, he returned home, where he learned that his grandmother had died and his five siblings had left the village.

Like most of his village, Madondo believed in ancestor worship. When his grandmother died, he pieced together what little money he could to buy a goat for a traditional sacrifice. He believed this would send her spirit peacefully into the world of the dead, and he hoped that her spirit in return would bring him blessing and good fortune. Looking back now, he saw the irony in those hopes. For the next ten years after the sacrifice, he told me, "Problems were falling on me all over. I was living in difficulty."

> *"Some people see us and say, 'If you are poor, you are not with Jesus, because Jesus would make you rich.'"*

Eventually an uncle helped him find work in Johannesburg. He borrowed a friend's ID book to sign for the job. In a few years he had started his own tiny shop selling cigarettes and snacks. By now the struggle against apartheid was at its height, and riots and strikes were common in South Africa, along with violence between political parties in the township. Madondo recalled walking for miles when the trains that carried people from black townships to factories went on strike, and fearing for his life if he hinted at a political opinion of any sort.

It was around this time that Madondo became a Christian. In his simple words, "I repented to Jesus, and fortunately Jesus saved my life." That was when, within a month of deciding to give Jesus his life, Madondo lost his job. He and his wife returned to their village empty-handed.

Like many people in his village, he farmed about four acres of land near his house. The first season after he returned from the city, his farming results were miserable. Only one strip of land yielded a few sacks of corn, and the rest were sparse. Such a meager harvest would not provide enough food for the year, much less seeds for the coming year. In his words, "These things didn't matter, though, because the Holy Spirit was still with me." During the long hungry winter and time of waiting for another small harvest, Madondo and his wife learned to cry to Jesus.

As I looked up from my notebook at the fields of beans and corn, I thought of the parable of the soils, where Jesus uses a farmer's field to illustrate why some people who hear about Jesus give up on their faith (see Mark 4:1–20). In rocky soil, seeds grow shallow roots and die in the sun. Other seeds are eaten by birds, and others are choked out by weeds, but the portion of the seeds that fell on good soil produced a harvest many times as great as the seeds that were sown. Here was a man whose newly sprouted faith faced all the dangers of life in the world—worries and hardship landed smack on a faith that had still only received a tiny bit of biblical teaching. Where some people would have let troubles and poverty choke away their faith, Madondo stayed focused on Christ.

"Even now," Madondo told me, "some people see us and say, 'If you are poor, you are not with Jesus, because Jesus would make you rich.' That's like saying to God, 'You failed me.'" He was growing in intensity, but carefully controlling the roll of his words like a Zulu preacher building to a climax.

"Just because someone is blessed with wealth doesn't mean he is blessed in his heart. God is not thinking like us— He always does things His own way. In those years when I had nothing, I realized this: God was training me to not just follow the blessings of God but to follow God. To know Jesus—that's a blessing!"

I smiled as he drove home his point. "You see," he continued, "I am very happy because I work for God. Even when there is no money, God can pay me. Everything we have, it comes from God. I talk lies if I say we are poor here." From inside the house I could hear gospel music playing on his stereo, one of the only signs of wealth in Madondo's homestead. It had been a long road to have even consistent food for his family, much less a stereo.

Ironically, God provided Madondo a way out of poverty

through good soil. While he had his monthly food gift from the neighboring village pastor, he still craved an answer to the puzzle of why some of his soil produced so little and some did well. He approached the department of agriculture and convinced them to do workshops for the farmers in his village. In the coming years, Madondo persuaded universities to conduct research and training in his remote village. He learned no-till planting methods, soil acidity testing, and other ways to maximize production in his plot. He diversified his homestead with cabbages, tomatoes, and spinach, and learned to mix and rotate legumes with other crops to keep nutrients in the soil. His crop yields went from less than one metric ton of corn harvested per year to seven or eight tons.

Soon he was elected a leader among the farmers of his village. He began receiving invitations from villages for miles around to do training workshops on gardening and agriculture. One organization hired him part-time. He was chosen to attend workshops in Zimbabwe and Uganda, and received a scholarship to finish a high school equivalency and begin a bachelor's degree in agriculture. "Just look at me," he marveled. "I dropped out of school in sixth grade, and now God has sent me to university."

With Madondo's skills and teaching experience, I could imagine him easily qualifying for a well-paying job in an urban central office of the department of agriculture, joining the thousands of gifted African leaders moving to cities each year. "So when you finish your university degree," I asked, "what are you going to do, find a big job in Johannesburg?"

"I don't even dream of it," he said soberly.

While his fields were bearing more and more physical fruit, what kept Madondo in his community was the spiritual fruit he saw growing there. Even the influence he gained as an agricultural presenter became a tool to reach the eternal realities of life.

"God has given me the gift of preaching," he told me. "And I have to use it." He described how he ran a recent weeklong visit to another village to train farmers in organic farming techniques. "Every day, I would preach first, then teach. Preach, then teach. On the last day, a man from the department of agriculture came, and he started the day, so I could not preach. By lunchtime, I felt too uneasy. The Holy Spirit said to me, 'Do not leave this village without giving them the blessing I prepared for them.' So when my turn came to teach, with that department of agriculture man listening, I preached. I told them about the mercy of Jesus, and many people were very touched, even healed. Some of them took me to their homes, and I prayed with them."

I watched Madondo greet individual students with a friendly rapport, asking about their families, their studies, and their dreams.

Madondo was working with human soil: churning in compost, hoeing and planting spiritual seeds to grow an eternal crop.

"When I pray with someone," he went on, "if I see that they don't have food or shoes, I don't just pray, I give them something. I know that whatever I give, it comes back multiplied, just not always in money. I want people to see my generosity and say, 'If I become a Christian, I want to be like this man.'"

Madondo had suffered through lean years learning to trust God in all situations, but he refused to stand by while his neighbors endured hardship. By his invitation, churches from nearby cities have donated clothing to his neediest neighbors, Christian projects have brought programs that support orphans, and nonprofit organizations have brought services such as adult education. When I mentioned to Madondo that I worked with a business development project, he clasped his hands together as his eyes grew wide.

"I have been praying for just something like that to come." He explained that he had tried already to organize community members to start small businesses and to save money for their children to go to college. After a year, though, nearly all the businesses were selling the same couple of products, and hardly anyone had any savings.

He arranged a meeting at the high school and offered to serve as my translator. When I had finished explaining the project, he launched into his own summary of the merits of running businesses. Soon his summary transitioned from a secular talk about business to a motivational sermon about using the opportunities God gives.

Most of the meeting attendees were students. I watched their faces, expecting them to roll their eyes at his sermon. Instead they were laughing, nodding, and interjecting encouragement. After the talk I watched Madondo greet individual students with a friendly rapport, asking about their families, their studies, and their dreams.

As much as I enjoyed working with Madondo, he was already overcommitted to projects, and no one else was stepping forward to train as staff for our organization. Besides that, our project required loan recipients to deposit loan payments into a bank, and the nearest bank was more than a thirty-minute bus ride away. Eventually we decided that expanding our project to the village was not feasible.

Madondo was disappointed, but as usual, he did not give up. A few months later he heard about another project that taught a group savings method to villagers instead of offering loans. The idea clicked perfectly with their needs. Villagers bought "shares" into a group by saving in one hundred rand (about eight dollar) increments. Provided the group had the money, they could then borrow up to three times what they had saved, and pay it back over any length of time agreed on by the group. Madondo had put in over three hundred dollars of savings into his group and had borrowed and paid back twice that for a building project on his house. Within two years, three groups of about fifteen people began operating in the village.

Like many of Madondo's attempts at improving his village, spreading money management skills had taken several tries. He had seen plenty of withered dreams along with successes. When I first interviewed Madondo, he was struggling to start a church. He told me that hardly anyone was attending, but he made no apologies. He said simply, "The devil is strong, I'm telling you, which means that we need to pray a lot."

Caring desperately for a community was often a thankless position. "My wife asks why I do it. Many times even the people I'm trying to help are against me."

"I tell her, 'My wife, when I'm sleeping, there's something lingering in my heart, that I must help my community.'"

He saw firsthand how people resisted change. "No one wants to try something else." When he had tried to start a soup kitchen, nearly every volunteer dropped out except his wife. Meanwhile many people were giving up planting with the new techniques that the university programs introduced. Some turned to growing marijuana, a high-profit crop that took minimal work. Madondo pointed out to farmer after farmer that many young people picked the weed and smoked it. "Money is good, but we're killing our kids.

"Many of the techniques we teach require more work, so people run away," he told me. "Sustainability is a hard word."

For Madondo there was no trip home to a foreign country, no perks, and often no pay. While some neighbors were turning back to their animal plows because they tired of the work, Madondo had his hands in both spiritual and physical dirt, carefully planning, making choices for the long haul. He set every one of his challenges before God just as he told his wife to set out their empty dishes.

One year later I visited Madondo again and asked about Madondo's church. "I'm so blessed," he said. "We meet every week, and we are always growing." Here was a man who worked in the dirt—he knew dirt intimately, and he made it grow things.

QUESTIONS *for discussion and reflection:*

1. Did Madondo's faith help him gain financial prosperity? Why or why not?

2. A common strain of teaching in churches across Africa, as well as elsewhere in the world, stresses that Christians should claim God's promises of material blessings. What are the pitfalls of this view of Christian life?

3. Read Proverbs 30:8–9:

   Give me neither poverty nor riches,
   But give me only my daily bread.
   Otherwise, I may have too much and disown you
   and say, "Who is the Lord?"
   Or I may become poor and steal,
   and so dishonor the name of my God.

   How has God answered this prayer in Madondo's life? Take time to meditate on this prayer both for your own life and for the world.

4. What did Madondo give up by staying in his home village? What did he gain?
5. Why do you think men in villages like Madondo's tend toward depression, spousal and child abuse, and spending the little money they have on alcohol or marijuana? In what ways can men in poverty be given dignity and self-respect?
6. Where in your community could you play a part in building the kingdom of God? Would it be easier for you to invest more deeply in serving where you are living now, or move elsewhere? To which do you sense God leading you?

MIXING AND
MANGLING: ERNEST

My questions began with frogs.

Phoebe and Zeke were playing outside the home of a ten-year-old Zulu friend when Phoebe spotted a frog nestled in the tall grass along their fence. Phoebe reached out a hand to grab it.

"No! No! Don't touch the frog!" The sound of their friend shouting drew me and his mother outside. Phoebe and Zeke mutely stepped backward, but I felt the need to find out more from their mother when we returned to our tea inside.

"Why do Zulu people not touch frogs?" I asked. I had heard pieces of explanations from others. Frogs, I had heard, had something to do with curses.

She paused, then spoke carefully. "People say they will do this—" She waved her hands and scrunched up her face as if to show something shooting from the frog into her face. "They will give you the face of a frog." She stopped as if thinking how to continue. "Do white people believe that?"

I told her no, but I mentioned the childhood tale that touching a toad would give you warts.

She did not smile. "This is different, I think." She spoke quietly, as if hiding secrets from some invisible listener. When she continued, she slipped into Zulu. My comprehension dropped to about 75 percent in Zulu, but it seemed she had no words in English for what she wanted to tell.

We sat across from each other at her kitchen table as she described in hushed tones the *sangomas*, the traditional medicine givers and spiritual guides. She said they could place a curse on a frog, and the frog would carry it to other people. She went on, describing how *sangomas* made "medicines" for all kinds of purposes. There were medicines to place in the corners of a new house to protect it from evil spirits and medicines to call on powers from deceased ancestors.

Meanwhile the three children squatted outside in a line, a few feet back from the frog, staring right back at the warty little creature.

It was not the first time we bumped into traditional Zulu beliefs, nor was it the last. We accepted an invitation to a party only to arrive and discover the occasion for the celebration was slaughtering a cow to send a dead person's spirit into another world, while a line of men sat on chairs making bawdy comments and drinking homemade Zulu beer. (Adam sat with the men for a few minutes, just long enough to taste the beer and hear a confusing explanation that it was made by grannies chewing up corn, spitting it out in water, and leaving it to ferment!) I met children who wore strings threaded with a bead or two tied around their waists to ward off evil. I saw scars on adults' faces, necks, and fingers where traditional healers had sliced in medicines to ward off spirits or identify a person's family lineage. A teenager once explained to me that he regularly drank traditional medicines that caused him to vomit out symbolic or real "snakes" as a way of purging himself of sins.

And then one day as we sat with friends at the little meat shop in the center of Amangwe eating cheap roast-your-own steaks and watching Zeke chase chickens around a woodpile, a stranger walked up to our bench. As I cut a slab of meat into bite-sized pieces for the kids, I overheard bits of the conversation between Adam and the man, and watched them exchange phone numbers before the stranger left.

"Well, that was different," Adam said as he sliced into his now cool meat. "He wants to give me Zulu lessons. And he's a *sangoma*."

Among foreigners and some South Africans, I heard *sangoma* translated as "witch doctor," but that translation had a history of being used with judgmental and insensitive connotations. What the day-to-day work of a *sangoma* was in modern-day South Africa I had no idea, but I couldn't resist the opportunity to find out. A few weeks later I called the number Adam had saved, explained that I was Adam's wife and a writer, and asked if I could interview him.

He certainly did not fit the witch doctor stereotype of a creepy old man throwing bones in a fire or cutting open sheep livers to tell fortunes.

And so it was that one afternoon I sat with some trepidation inside the eight-foot square office of a *sangoma*, receiving an education on Zulu beliefs from frogs to the afterlife. I brought along a friend visiting from the United States, in part because he shared my curiosity and writing interests and in part because Adam had warned that this might be an interview worth having an extra presence along for the sake of "safety." Whether he meant safety in the physical realm or the spiritual, I wasn't quite sure, but I took his advice.

"Some frogs are just frogs." The *sangoma* smiled his huge winning smile; long eyelashes brightened his whole face. He was thirty-one-years old, went by the English name Ernest, spoke impeccable English, and certainly did not fit the witch doctor stereotype of a creepy old man throwing bones in a fire or cutting open sheep livers to tell fortunes.

"But other frogs," he continued, "are sent by *umthakathi* [pronounced "oom-tah-**kah**-tee"] and they are *thokolosha*" [pronounced "toe-go-**low**-sha"].

These were words I needed to be defined, but Ernest was patient while I scribbled notes. What I would do with the notes I wasn't sure. As a North American, I had never taken time to work out a theology of witchcraft, and I was not sure I could interest many North American Christian readers in the topic either. The answers seemed clear enough that, quite simply, it was wrong. I was quickly learning, though, that for Ernest and for many South African Christians and non-Christians alike, it was not simple at all.

An *umthakathi*, Ernest said, is roughly what we would call a witch. By his description they were people without scruples who would curse people even to the point of aiming to kill. Often they earned a living by this work, but an ordinary person could also act as an *umthakathi* by calling on spiritual powers. They conjured up curses, or *thokolosha*, which could take physical forms like lightning, dwarves, snakes . . . or frogs.

"I am not an *umthakathi*," he went on. "In my beliefs you should not kill someone. I am a Christian. "

My friend and I had agreed before the interview to let Ernest speak without judging or debating. We would save the most controversial questions for last and let Ernest explain his views of reality before we offered ours. I stifled my surprise and skepticism at Ernest's claim to be a Christian and let him explain.

"I have three jobs," he said. "First, I am a prophet, which means I communicate with God. Second, I am an *inyanga*, which is a traditional healer. And third, I am also a *sangoma*— a spiritual guide. I believe in God, and I am only here to help people and to heal the sick."

The walls were lined with shelves of jars, each labeled with Zulu words I didn't recognize and filled with what looked like a variety of spices and herbs. Outside an old man pounded a log into a can filled with something like bark. The man poured out piles of whatever he was crushing onto newspapers as if to dry in the sunlight. On a bench nearby, the first customers of the day lined up waiting.

"I heal using these things, but it is just another way of healing." Ernest showed us the jars of herbs for strokes, epilepsy, and other illnesses. Some were taken as teas; others burned and the smoke inhaled. Others were merely to be placed strategically, like the sachets deposited in each corner of a new house to protect against sickness and other disaster.

"In a way, my work is like Jesus. You know the story of how Jesus put mud on a blind man's eyes to heal him?" I nodded that I knew the story, hoping the nod didn't convey that I agreed that how he healed was just like how Jesus healed. I still had a lot of questions about whether the power he used to heal had anything to do with Jesus.

Ernest was articulate, energetic, and locally renowned for his skills. I couldn't help thinking that he regarded his healing practice similarly to most doctors I knew. His family survived on what customers paid for his services, and he saw his medical services as a business.

The obvious question, in this province of South Africa with a sky-high HIV rate, was what he thought about HIV. He didn't shy away from the question. "The way to avoid HIV is through condoms, safe sex, and abstinence." He knew it was not caused by evil spirits, he knew the book answers, and he told them to his customers.

He confirmed, though, what I had heard even from teachers and educated people in the area: other traditional healers would give different responses. Some claimed to have herbs or powers that could cure HIV. "They say they can cure HIV," Ernest said, "but they lie."

He pulled out a large jar of mixed herbs, labeled *Ingculaza* ("eeng-tsu-lah-za").[7] "This one I use to treat HIV. I treat it, but I can't heal it." It reminded me of doctors giving out vitamins and encouraging a balanced meal to prolong the health of an HIV-positive patient, and yet I suspected there was a deeper significance to those herbs than what a Westerner would see in a bottle of vitamins.

"To heal, it has to be given to you to heal," he said. "If a person is about to die, it's his days."

My friend asked, "So what do you do when it's 'his days' to die?"

Ernest said he would tell patients to try a doctor. "We are different. They're using stuff we don't know." He didn't disrespect doctors, he just saw his own calling differently.

Ernest showed us the beads he tied around a baby's wrist to prevent teething infections and the razor blades with which he cut people to put herbs in their blood (he insisted in these days of HIV, he never used the same razor blade twice).

For our Western way of thinking, this was a whole new view of reality. Enough studies had been done to show the validity of some traditional remedies of various cultures from Chinese to Native American that I would not argue about whether some of these herbs might have healing properties, but when it came to spiritual questions, the stakes got higher. His work was more than physical healing and herbal teas. He also showed us the yarn he tied around a person's waist to protect them from evil, saying, "You must pray to this." For a *sangoma*, he said, the spiritual risks were even fiercer, so he posted four white flags around his home, to which he prayed for protection from harmful spirits. And we had not talked to him long before the discussion led to ancestors.

Ernest explained that his job was more than just a traditional healer. His job was also to consult the ancestors. People came to him with questions on everything from relationships to wealth, and he looked to the ancestors for wisdom. This included silent prayer to them as he worked, trances, séances, and ceremonies like the cow sacrifice we had found ourselves attending.

When I asked how Ernest became a *sangoma*, he explained, "I was quite young—too young—when I started to be a prophet. While I was in my church, I was shocked when something came to me."

This "something," he believed, was "the Spirit of the almighty God." He said, "After that, I could see some things." By his final year in high school, he believed his ancestors were speaking to him clearly and strongly. "Inside the classroom, I would cry not knowing what was happening to me."

In the following years, Ernest consulted other *sangomas* for training and continued listening to his ancestors. "In dreams, ancestors come to me to tell me about herbs to heal the people. I get some herbs from mountains. I dig them. I get them from trees. I travel a lot, and other people give some to me." But when it came to healing, he said he only healed when the ancestors told him how. He also shared that during his training as a *sangoma*, he was one of the only learners who prayed to God. His trainers had not encouraged this, and even implied that it was a "dangerous" habit for him, but in his heart, he continued praying to God.

"I am a Christian. But there are a lot of differences between what I believe and what you believe. We believe in ancestors."

115

"I am a Christian," he declared. "But there are a lot of differences between what I believe and what you believe. We in South Africa believe in ancestors."

In his belief system, a person hoped to be welcomed into "the family of ancestors" after death. If someone's sins were too great, it could take consulting the ancestors (through a *sangoma* like himself) to reveal the deceased person's sins. Then it was the responsibility of living family members to perform ceremonies like slaughtering a cow or goats in order to "wash away" the deceased relative's sins. If the sacrifice was acceptable, the ancestors forgave the sins and welcomed the deceased into their family.

Once they were welcomed into the ancestral family, the ancestors appeared to have a fair amount of wisdom or power. But Ernest insisted, "I don't pray to ancestors; I talk to them." He explained that the forgiveness of God came separately from the forgiveness of ancestors, but he did not mention Jesus as bringing this forgiveness.

I had seen the burden put on society by a belief system that said honoring one's ancestors determined one's success in life. I had heard Zulu friends explain that as soon as a person rejects the ceremonies for ancestors, their neighbors point fingers at every problem in their lives, saying, "That's because you angered your ancestors." When people suffered from recurring illnesses as with HIV, their neighbors often claimed they either had received a curse or were being punished by ancestors, which led to shunning and stigma. One woman I knew went so far as to dig her daughter's body from the ground to rebury it in a way that would please the dead girl's spirit. One of her Christian family members was appalled, and called the police in tears to stop the ceremony.

In English, Ernest used the word God, but in Zulu he used a word unfamiliar to me. He explained that early white missionaries brought the word for God I was used to: *"Nku-lunkulu"* ("n-koo-loon-koo-loo," pronounced with a quiet "n" sound at the beginning), meaning literally "The Great, Great One." He used an older word: *Umvelinqanyi* ("oom-vay-leen-*k*ah-nee "),[8] meaning "The One Who Was at the Beginning."

The line of customers outside had grown to twice the length of the benches where the first dozen sat. We thanked Ernest for his time, and as we left he invited us to visit the church that met next door to his *sangoma* office.

I drove home with my mind bubbling with questions and my stomach tight with uneasiness. A question about frogs had opened a whole can of worms. Since the time of my first interest in Africa, which grew as I studied traditional stories from across the continent, I had wanted to exist in this country primarily as a listener and a learner, and only secondly as a teacher. But as a listener whose authority came from Christ, I needed to step back and interpret what I had heard. I recalled the Bible's warning that Satan's servants "masquerade as servants of righteousness" (2 Corinthians 11:15). What ancient practices could be redeemed, and what must be thrown out? Could I trust that the God he prayed to, this *Umvelinqanyi*, was the same as the God I followed? For all his profession of faith, where did his supposed powers come from? What about this practice of speaking with ancestors? These were questions I had never asked in the North American church where I was raised.

I was amazed at the courage it took for him to speak to me so freely. By his belief system, our conversation could be heard by the "unseen spies" of the spiritual realm, and he would have to answer for their displeasure if they disapproved of what he shared with me. What were his motives to talk with me? Did he merely want the status of having a foreigner in his home and church? Did he expect to gain some power over me, or was he hoping for financial benefit?

In South Africa, as in much of the continent, mixing pieces of Christianity and traditional beliefs, a phenomenon called syncretism, was widespread. Throw in the occasional teachings of a recent spiritual leader claiming to be a messenger from God, and you have a spectrum including everyone from the frog-cursers, to Ernest, to mainline international denominations all using the same word "Christian" with very different definitions.

"People do foolishness with these ancestor spirits too much," she said in Zulu.

A common quality of most of the traditional religions that preceded Christianity in the continent of Africa was a practice of trying whatever works whenever it works. There were and still are few written or permanent codes of behavior or traditional religious practice, so each local spiritual leader could to some extent try one explanation for reality and when that fails, try another. When the first Christian missionaries arrived, Christianity became just the latest trick to try, and when the newly defined god didn't behave as they hoped, they could shuffle back in some traditional ceremonies until something worked.

I contemplated Ernest's invitation to his church, wondering what my Zulu friends would think if I accepted it. I wanted their advice in sorting through a correct response to this local belief system, and yet I suspected a lot of South African Christians would flat out disapprove of ever setting foot on this man's property again.

In fact as I thought about who might have insight into this Christian-traditional-mix religion, I could not think of a single evangelical Christian of any race who I could imagine even holding a conversation with a *sangoma* about their faith. A white South African woman had told me once that every time she drove the highway through Amangwe, she prayed that evil spirits would be dispersed, but she stressed that she would never stop her car there. A Zulu pastor who heard we were thinking of visiting Ernest's church expressed concern that I would be sending the wrong impression by being seen on Ernest's property. I understood the pastor's concern. I could walk in, hear Ernest's story, and leave the area without having to deal with the fallout of whatever unintentional messages my visit sent.

After the interview, when I mentioned to a Zulu Christian friend that I was talking to a *sangoma*, she tilted her head and stared at me as if she thought I was lucky to have escaped picking up some kind of curse—in the same way I would catch a cold.

"What do you think of the traditional beliefs?" I pressed her.

"People do foolishness with these ancestor spirits too much," she said in Zulu. Her word for "foolishness" was the same that mothers used to describe their children's misbehavior when a spanking was swift to follow, like if a child climbed up a cabinet of glass jars. "The more they fool around with them, the more they're going to be hurt by those same spirits."

Soon we were paging through Zulu and English Bibles finding verses like "This is how you can recognize the Spirit of God: Every spirit that acknowledges that Jesus Christ has come in the flesh is from God" (1 John 4:2).

That was a start, but with Ernest's mixed-up profession of faith in Jesus plus reliance on ancestors, I needed more specifics.

As my friend and I paged through the Old Testament, I realized that these issues were as old as the Bible. The laws given to Moses clearly spelled out "Let no one be found among you who . . . practices divination or sorcery, interprets omens, engages in witchcraft, or casts spells, or who is a medium or spiritist or who consults the dead. Anyone who does these things is detestable to the Lord, and because of these detestable practices the Lord your God will drive out those nations before you. You must be blameless before the Lord your God" (Deuteronomy 18:10–13; also see Leviticus 19:26, 31).

Many hundred years later in the New Testament, I read about early Christians confronting questions of culture again. Now, though, they had the added insight that Jesus had come to justify and save people of all nations. Christ was promised as the "desired of all nations" (Haggai 2:7) and commanded His followers that after He left them they must "go and make disciples of all nations" (Matthew 28:19). That was a very good thing for all of us, I realized, since most Christians, myself included, come from people groups who were once at least as far from Christianity as *sangomas* appear to us today.

As I thought about how to respond to Ernest, I remembered a fairy tale story that Phoebe had recently made up and illustrated. Like most of her favorite stories, her tale included a witch. At the end of the story, though, the heroic children of the story did not destroy the witch or chase her off a cliff. Instead the last page showed a colorful drawing of several smiling stick figures holding stick hands, with the words "then the children taught the witch how to be nice, and then they were all friends."

That was the kind of fairy tale ending I wanted for the people of Amangwe. I didn't want the people that outsiders called "witch doctors" to be destroyed or ostracized. I wanted an ending where someone taught these traditional spiritual leaders a better way. I couldn't see any hope of changing traditional beliefs if all of the Christians swore not to be seen speaking to any *sangomas*, and I therefore couldn't turn down an invitation to visit Ernest again.

So Adam and the children and I went to visit Ernest's church. Aside from most of the members wearing blue robes and taking off their shoes before entering the little shack of a church building, the service began much like the Christian Zulu church we attended. They sang songs a cappella, some of which I recognized, and then everyone prayed out loud at the same time. Then things got interesting. Most of the teenagers and adults began marching in a circle, taking turns spinning within the circle one after another while the congregation sang. Adam and I exchanged awed glances as the dancers spun faster and faster, the older ones and teenagers dropping out one by one until only the most skilled dancers remained. Finally Ernest danced alone, spinning for at least fifteen minutes more quickly and constantly than any ballet dancer I had ever seen. I expected a dramatic otherworldly ceremony to follow the spinning, but instead Ernest just finished suddenly, wiped sweat off his face, and continued the service with music and a prayer by a church member. He preached a noncontroversial sermon about being kind and generous and then asked Adam if he would like to say anything.

Adam rose to the occasion with a clear explanation of Jesus Christ as the Savior chosen by God for our sins. It was an indirectly ancestor-worship-challenging message about the sufficiency of Christ as a mediator between us and God, the only sacrifice we would ever need. Ernest translated accurately, the congregation listened silently, and when the service finished we parted ways with congeniality.

For the next half year, my notes from the interview with Ernest sat in my computer. I never finished an article about him, even though it remained on my list of chapters I hoped to include in this book. I struggled to write about him. I wanted a clear story line with a nice resolution. Living and writing in the in-betweens of life is never easy, but I made up my mind before writing this book that I would not shy away from the less-than-perfect stories because they are what makes up real life. We will never finish grappling with questions of culture. While there are definite rights and wrongs of what God commands for all cultures, there is also a long line of greys in between. We need to take time to listen and understand with compassion, not automatically condemn whatever strikes us as odd, from wearing too little clothing to nursing a child until he's four years old. As one of my favorite quotes about the task of a Christian in a foreign culture points out, "Missionary work, therefore, is a paradox: on the one hand, the missionary is required by natural law to respect the right of a people to its own culture and national character; on the other hand, he is commanded to transform the world."[9] While we do not need to focus, then, on external or "cosmetic" differences in cultural practice, we must wisely remain diligent to discern and respond to spiritual differences.

And so my husband and I continued the conversation with Ernest. He would call us from time to time, and we would stop in for visits. As I began writing this book, I stopped to visit his family one afternoon on the way to dinner with some friends. A wild thunderstorm hit the valley a half hour before I planned to leave for his home on my motorcycle, but the rain let up to a drizzle long enough for me to pull on rain gear and go. The visit soon became even more surreal than my first visit to his jar-filled office. Ernest, his wife, and I sat in his living room by candlelight at four o'clock in the afternoon while the occasional flash of lightning streaked past the window and waves of rain clattered on the tin roof.

To my surprise, in Ernest's first sentence past a greeting, he announced that he had bought a new keyboard to go with his "whole new church."

"Whole new church?" I asked. "What kind of church?"

"Like yours. Just a church. A real church."

I eyed him suspiciously. My faith struggled to keep up with what appeared to be reality, that Ernest had scrapped the old syncretistic church and fully given his life to Jesus Christ. He was not wearing his *sangoma* doctor's coat, and I had noticed that his old one-room cinderblock church building had been dismantled. I had come mentally armed with all the Bible verses I had been digging up since my first interview with Ernest, but maybe I wouldn't need any of them.

"What I do is my culture," Ernest said. "I can't go against my culture." "But Christians in any culture have to go against their culture," I said.

"So . . ." I proceeded cautiously. "Let me ask it this way. You know I'm working on a book. You know a lot of people probably think I'm crazy for going to visit you, like I should be afraid of you. But I feel like people should hear what you think. But Ernest, people will want to know if you're really a Christian. So what should I tell them?"

The question was out, and he began to pour out argument after argument that there was no difference between his faith and mine. But the more he defended his faith, the more I worried. The conversation soon returned to ancestor worship, and on that point we simply could not agree. I pointed out the Scriptures my Christian friends and I had found, and he argued around them. My watch reminded me that my friends would be waiting for me, but I decided to give the weather another half hour and see if I might catch a break in the rain.

"What I do is my culture," Ernest said. "I can't go against my culture."

"But Christians in any culture have to go against their culture," I said. "I have to go against my culture when it tells me that in times of trouble I should rely on money, jobs, lawyers, medicine, and entertainment instead of God. It's no different from your culture telling you to go to ancestors in times of trouble. It comes down to choosing to trust God first, 100 percent, all the time, no matter what."

Ernest's wife, who didn't understand English well enough to keep up with the conversation, slipped out to give her youngest son a bath in a plastic tub in the bedroom.

Ernest glanced over his shoulder at them as they left.

"Look," he said gently. "I'm not saying I want to practice as a *sangoma* anymore. I'm tired of it in fact. But I don't know what else to do. How else am I going to feed my family? I didn't even finish high school. Look at my children. I tell you it's hard to see them hungry and know there's nothing to give them. It's terrible. You understand that?"

I imagined Phoebe or Zeke growing thin and weak as they whined day after day for food. I imagined having no food in our cupboards, nothing, not just a shortage of snacks like crackers and peanut butter, but having no bread, fruit, vegetables, rice, beans, or flour.

"I have never been there," I said quietly. "But I know people who have." I described to him how Madondo and his wife had suffered in their early years as Christians.

"I tell you." Ernest shook his head. "There are pastors who preach that these traditional ways are wrong. They say they will never offer sacrifices to ancestors or consult them. But they do it. They all do it. I know a pastor who had a chicken passed in to him through a window in the middle of the night so he could sacrifice it."

I tried to focus on the issue at stake without being distracted by the absurd (but possibly true) image of a Zulu pastor receiving a live chicken through a window by moonlight.

"First Ernest," I said, leaning forward toward him, looking him straight in the eye, "even if they are all doing it, it doesn't mean it's right. They might also be gossiping, sleeping with ten women, or beating their wives. But that doesn't make it right. And secondly Ernest . . ." I paused and shook my head, praying he could believe what I said. "They do not all do it. And the ones who do not, the ones who trust in God only and in nothing else, their lives are blessed because of it."

"Blessed?" He opened his arms. "What about this couch? What about the keyboard? The television? Do they have these?" Since I had last visited, he had purchased all of these, including the huge plush couches that we sat on. His definition of blessing was the opposite of Madondo's.

"You know," he continued, "many people who had stopped believing in traditional healers are coming back these days. There are a lot of problems and illnesses in our communities that are not solved by doctors or anyone else." HIV was spreading faster than people's understanding of its symptoms and prognosis could catch up. Unless people swallowed the stigma and got tested, got treatment, and stuck to their treatment regimen, people would watch their bodies fall into sickness after sickness with mysteriously increasing frequency. And in times of trouble, they fell back on their deepest roots. For many Zulu people, this meant *sangomas*.

My cell phone rang. The friends I was meeting for dinner suggested that they meet me halfway with their four-by-four truck to drive me up their slick driveway in the rain, which had not let up.

In the end, Ernest and I agreed to disagree. As we said good-bye, he told me he wanted to attend seminary and asked if I knew of any. I gladly told him the name of a reputable one where I knew African professors would stand up against ancestor-worshiping practices. I also gave him the name of a quality Zulu pastor I knew in the area and promised to arrange a meeting between the two of them.

It was already dark when I climbed onto my motorcycle. The rain had slowed to a drizzle, but I knew it would be a slippery and slow ride to meet my friends and park the motorcycle with some friends on the way to their home. As I turned the key and the headlight shone into the darkness, I replayed the last piece of conversation Ernest and I had shared. Compared to many places, South Africa was a relatively easy place to become a Christian. If Ernest gave up his *sangoma* practice, he might face a few angry clients, and there was of course the lost income issue, but he would probably not have the kind of threats on his life or complete ostracizing that would face new Christians in other parts of the world.

I also knew, though, that giving up a cultural idol is not easy, whatever the culture. The amazing thing is that people can manage to give up those idols with God's loving help. Throughout history, people have peeked into a new way of seeing reality, felt a tug from a real God who loves them, and made the leap into His arms. Following Jesus is perfectly simple—we don't need any special résumé of good deeds or proof of a certain bloodline—but it also requires absolutely everything from us. It begins with a full-body swan dive or cannonball jump into the washing of Christ's forgiving love, and then it continues in every little decision of every day. Early Christians grappled with questions like what to do with a sorcerer who asked them to bless his ministry, whether to eat food that had been dedicated to idols, and whether every follower of Christ needed to be circumcised like the Jews. And anyone who follows Christ today, whether Ethiopian, Italian, Costa Rican, Iranian, Malaysian, or North American, faces their own serious choices, some even more difficult than whether to touch the frogs.

QUESTIONS *for discussion and reflection:*

1. Why is it important that foreigners, particularly missionaries and evangelists, be sensitive to maintaining aspects of a person's culture?

2. If you knew someone in your own culture who had just become a Christian, how would you help them determine the line between what cultural norms should be challenged or eliminated, and what should be preserved or adapted? How would you determine that line in another culture?

3. What unique challenges does a foreigner—as opposed to someone from the local culture—face in speaking to someone about their beliefs?

4. Imagine you are speaking to Ernest. How would you make a convincing but culturally appropriate explanation of why ancestor worship is incompatible with Christianity?

5. What idols are you tempted to rely on in your culture? Now make a culturally appropriate explanation of why those idols of your own culture are incompatible with Christianity.

JUST IN TIME:
PHAKAMILE

"Where are you?"

My friend Roz was on the phone. She was supposed to meet me in ten minutes to take my car to a mechanic. There was no way I would make it. "How long can you wait?"

"I'll run errands in town. It's fine." Her voice said it was not. "How long will you be?"

I hated questions like these. My life of deadlines and time estimates mixed like oil in water with the unpredictability of life in the developing world.

"I'll hurry." I slipped the cell phone deep in a pocket and winced at the obstacle course before me.

I was carrying Zeke on one hip while Phoebe pressed into my other side. We walked single file behind a South African grandmother named Pabble who hobbled along on ankles swollen to the size of my thighs, down a path that twisted between scrub brush and a barbed wire fence. Ten meters ahead, a trench of greenish water from a nearby farm made a six-foot-wide furrow intersecting our path. I saw only one bridge spanning the gap: two lines of corrugated tin, a few inches wide each, placed shoulder width apart. That was the only way to Phakamile's house.

The day before had been one of my weekly errand-running days jam-packed with grocery, hardware, butcher, library, and bank stops in the company of my two dawdling and whining children. As we stepped out of the grocery store, Zeke noticed Sofi's vehicle a few spaces down the street and shouted, "Doong's here!" I explained that Doong was in school, but I spotted Sofi's face through the pharmacy window.

It was not often that I saw Sofi overwhelmed, but there she was, crying in the pharmacy. "There's nothing the doctor can do for her," she croaked when we popped in to say hello.

I reached out an arm for a side-hug and waited for her sniffles to subside.

"You got a minute?" she asked without waiting for an answer. "Come help me get this woman home."

I tucked the children back into the car with library books while Sofi made her purchases, and then followed Sofi next door to the doctor's office.

Inside, the woman Sofi spoke of sat waiting, a bent lump moaning quietly. Beneath a white cloth, unchecked cancer had eaten away one breast and burrowed a fist-sized hole into her chest. Her arm was swollen to the point of cracking the skin, and puss oozed from her open sore. She raised hollow eyes to us when Sofi gently spoke her name—Phakamile.

"Can't we visit her tomorrow?" Phoebe insisted. "Maybe we could bring her some food if she doesn't have any to give us."

I helped Sofi lift the emaciated women into her truck. As I climbed into my own car, Phoebe asked quietly, "What about the sick lady? Are we going to visit her?"

My thoughts churned over the list of errands remaining for the morning. "Honey, we don't have time today. Sofi will take her home."

"Do you think she'll be better soon? Is it the kind of sick

like when you throw up?" Phoebe had long since forgotten the feeling of breaking a bone, but she had just gotten over a bout of the flu, lying motionless on our couch for hours at a time and vomiting a few times a day. That was about the worst thing she could imagine.

"No it isn't that." I chose not to explain that in fact she might throw up a lot, but if she threw up, it was from the pain and the fact that her insides were being eaten up by a thing called cancer, and very likely she also had a thing called AIDS that keeps your body from being able to get better from even simple things like the flu. Instead I calmly explained that it probably was a sickness that wouldn't get better, and she would be sick until she died.

"Can't we visit her tomorrow?" Phoebe insisted. "Maybe we could bring her some food if she doesn't have any to give us. Maybe we could even have a sleepover. Maybe she has kids!"

Her spirit shone like a lightbulb. I turned and stared at her. This was supposed to be my one trip into town for the week, and another trip in this direction tomorrow was not in the plans. This afternoon I needed to spend time updating our accounting records and clean the house to have dinner with a group of expat friends. Then to my surprise, I remembered we did have a free morning and a reason to come into town tomorrow. I had been meaning to leave the car at the mechanic for some minor repairs. We could stop to visit Phakamile in the early morning, then catch a ride home from the mechanic with a friend who took her son to preschool. "Yes Phoebe, that's a great idea. Let's go visit the sick lady tomorrow." I could see the pieces fitting nicely in their places.

So here we were. There was nothing nice about this path, though. "It's easier through the barbed wire here," I said, setting Zeke down to let Pabble lean on my shoulder. She lifted a leg ever so slowly over the twisted wire. She was so deliberate, taking all the time I didn't have.

I had not invited her, just asked Sofi for directions to Phakamile's house and she told me to stop at her church to ask Pabble for directions. Instead of giving me directions, Pabble insisted on coming. As a "colored" person—from a mixed heritage of black, white, or Indian—she served in the Zulu community as a local missionary of the purest sort—loved talking about Jesus, volunteered nearly every day, spoke Zulu fluently.

I, on the other hand, could comprehend a fair amount of Zulu but usually only felt confident enough with my speaking to say simple sentences like "Your cow is large and nice." I figured I would show up, smile, and at most stumble through a few pages of the Zulu Bible. In fact I had not planned much at all.

This was his next-door neighbor. Had he never taken the time to cross into their world?

Pabble seemed not to have planned either. After our second time driving past the homestead where she thought Phakamile lived, I realized to my disgust that she did not know the way in. On my third time turning around, we spotted a man leaning over the engine of a tractor and pulled farther into the driveway to ask for directions.

I rolled down my window. "Do you know how to get to those huts over there?" I pointed across a field to what Pabble promised would be Phakamile's homestead.

"Don't know." He eyed us suspiciously. "There's a boy over there who works here."

I caught myself picturing a ten-year-old before I realized that his use of the word "boy" had nothing to do with age. The word passed over his lips as if it never occurred to him that it would offend anyone.

"In fact that's all my land, but I've never been down there. You can't drive your car through that fence." Then as if it excused his never having visited the family that shared his own property, he added, "They built that fence, not me."

I stared at him. This was his next-door neighbor. Members of her family worked for him. Had he never taken the time to cross into their world?

He climbed back on his tractor. Today he would plow that tractor through fields of corn and soybeans, not unlike any farm in my home state of Wisconsin. He could be my own neighbor or a fellow churchgoer. He could be me. I thought of neighbors I had never visited, people I had never spoken with about more than the weather and the ages of their children.

"There's a woman dying in there," Pabble said out her window as I pulled forward. In her voice was the determination of a woman who did not care who built the fence—she was finding a way through.

Following the man's driveway toward the fence took us through a virtual trash heap of discarded farm implements and boulders, and I cringed at every bump, imagining popping yet another tire or snapping something off the undercarriage of the car. At the fence we locked the car, then picked our way down along the fence to within sight of the line of three mud buildings. Now here I was facing the danger of dropping my children into a trench of greenish water.

Zeke whimpered and I told myself the house across the bridge was probably empty anyway. This was all seeming so ridiculous. Aside from my daughter's whim, I had no excuse to be here. This was far from my job as a small business trainer, and I had no notions of striking up any lasting friendship. Pabble carried only her Zulu Bible, and all that was in my backpack were my own Zulu Bible and the adult diapers and energy drink and porridge packs Sofi had handed me the night before. I checked my watch again, glanced behind to the path we had covered, then looked back at the bridge. If I crossed this bridge, there was no turning back without going in that house, and if I went in that house, there was no way I would return in time to make my appointment at the mechanic. "Pabble, we can try this another time."

Pabble turned and faced me, said nothing, and took another step toward the bridge.

Suddenly from behind us came the sound of sliding pebbles and a young Zulu man bounding the last few steps down the path to where we stood eyeing the bridge. After a short Zulu conversation with Pabble, he swept Phoebe into his arms and carried her across the bridge, his practiced legs maneuvering the steps easily.

Next went Pabble, trembling and clutching both the man's hands as he walked backwards in front of her.

Phoebe called me anxiously from where the man had set her, and before the man could return to help, I straddled one leg onto each thin band of metal and began the crossing. Whispering reassurances to Zeke and trying not to look down as the tin vibrated beneath my feet and the murky water between them widened, I commanded my feet to land in place, wider and wider, step by precarious step.

Across the bridge, I paused to look back at the bridge just long enough to feel my heart rate slowing toward normal. We ducked into the first mud house and found Phakamile propped on a mattress on the floor. Two women—I assumed Phakamile's mother and a sister—sat on the floor of the hut. A blanket lay loosely over Phakamile's shoulders. Phoebe sat down beside a boy of about her age, showing him pictures from the library book she had carried all the way there. I steered Zeke away from the smoldering fire in the middle of the room.

I sat beside Phakamile on the mattress, trying to act as if it were the most normal thing in the world to sit beside a half-dressed woman dying in a dirt-floor home. Now and then I joined her fingers as she tugged nervously at her grey blanket, pulling it over her shoulder again and again. Every few minutes it dropped again, revealing the gaping hole over her heart.

The two relatives listened intently while we demonstrated how to prepare the energy drink and porridge. Then Pabble opened her Bible, and somehow my sparse Zulu made sense of nearly every word. The familiar words she read from John 3:16 seemed to take on new life in Zulu. "God loved the world so much that He gave His only Son, so that . . ." So that Phakamile would not die but have eternal life. The words mingled with the smell of infection, the sight of Phoebe nearly sitting in the ashes of a dying fire reading a library book with Phakamile's son, and the sound of rhythmic moaning.

Did she really understand enough to make a choice to accept Jesus' death as a payment for her sins and enter a relationship with God for eternity?

"Repeat after me," Pabble insisted. Phakamile's eyes faded to the right and left, her head bobbing with a tearless crying sound. I placed my hand on her bare shoulder.

"Repeat this, Phakamile," Pabble called. "Phakamile!"

The woman's head lifted and faced Pabble. Her groans reminded me of the sounds I made giving birth to my children.

"Lord Jesus . . ." Pabble began to pray, and Phakamile muttered the words, barely remembering two words at a time, eyes glazed but blinking hungrily toward Pabble. "Forgive me Jesus . . . You love me . . ."

I watched Zeke patiently pulling kernels from a corncob that might have been the family's food for a day.

"*Ufile,*" Pabble was saying. *You died.*

The woman choked and her voice gave out.

"*Ufile!*" Pabble's voice rose louder in the smoky hut.

"*U—*" Again the woman's voice trailed off.

"*Ufile ngami!*" *You died for me.* I pressed gently on Phakamile's back, swaying in the rhythm of her breathing, and her words flowed out with all the emotion of a child being born: *You died for me.*

The day was windy and grey, unseasonably cold for spring. Later, back at home I would eat a cheese sandwich and taste only the smell of disease. I would sit next to Phoebe while she drew a picture, burst into tears myself when she became frustrated, and walk out of the house. I wandered toward our river. Crouched in the sand by the gurgling waterfall, I let my tears run.

As I stared into the churning water, I realized there was no way to know for sure what was going on in Phakamile's heart during our visit. Did she really understand enough of Pabble's words to make a choice to accept Jesus' death as a payment for her sins and enter a relationship with God for eternity? Or did she already know Christ as Lord, Savior, and friend before we came and our visit was just a repeat of what had already happened long ago between her and God?

But the strong possibility remained that Phakamile had not accepted Jesus before we came, and what we witnessed there was a genuine first conversation between her and God. Quite likely that three-hour chunk of time in my life overlapped with Phakamile joining the ranks of "whoever believes in Him," that she will now not perish but have eternal life.

Phakamile died two days later. For days the smell of death from that little hut haunted me, sometimes at every inhalation, sometimes in the middle of a bowl of macaroni. I wondered if for Phakamile's household that was the measure of how sweet was the smell of eternal life, a freshness that is supposed to hover like a cloud of perfume everywhere a Christian goes.

If Pabble and I had only brought diapers, porridge, and children's library books, it would not have made a lick of difference to Phakamile four days after our visit. I hardly spoke any words during the visit, and in fact the only part I played was deciding not to skip the whole visit, following the holy whim of my daughter and swallowing my fear of offending a friend waiting at the mechanic.

If Phakamile's untreated cancer was what it looked like to have a God-shaped hole in her heart, well, God fit in some pretty gory spaces. If God was going there, though, it was worth every effort to tag along.

QUESTIONS *for discussion and reflection:*

1. List the points in the story where the author wavered between visiting Phakamile or spending time elsewhere, and the excuses she had not to make the visit. In what ways do you cling to your own organization of your time?
2. What steps would you like to take toward letting God use your time however He wants?
3. Read from Romans 10:13–15; Paul is writing about people who, without someone telling them, may never have a chance to accept Jesus as Savior:

   "Everyone who calls on the name of the Lord will be saved." How, then, can they call on the one they have not believed in? And how can they believe in the one of whom they have not heard? And how can they hear without someone preaching to them? And how can they preach unless they are sent?

What does it mean to be "saved"? What leads to a person being saved?

4. Have you prayed a prayer similar to Phakamile's, accepting Jesus' death as a payment for your sins? Do you live in the freedom of knowing you will spend eternity with God?
5. How much of your time do you spend on activities that could make a difference in the eternal destiny of other people? How might God be challenging you to be more engaged in leading others to eternal salvation?

THE BLOOMING FLOWER
HOUSE: CHARMAINE

One morning, an American nurse named Jules visiting South Africa decided to take a different side road on her way home from the AIDS hospice where she had been volunteering. She had heard rumors of a woman, very sick, possibly abandoned, living down that road. Carefully steering her car over potholes and ruts as deep as her axles, Jules cringed at the memory of ripping off an oil pan on a similar road earlier that month. Around a few more bends of the road, she would discover that God was protecting more than her car that day.

Not a mile from the hospice, the road twisted and passed through a fence into a cultivated field. Just before the fence, shaded by woods and disappearing into overgrown elephant grass, a little one-room hut sat as if the house itself had been quarantined to the farthest edge of humanity. The nurse stopped the car and took the keys from the ignition. She paused, staring at the yard scattered with leaves and weeds, feeling a loneliness hovering over the house.

Inside, a woman's withered body lay on a bed. The woman was awake, though she did not know what time it was or how long she had slept, nor when she had last eaten. Over a month now, possibly. Her elderly mother brought water sometimes, poured slowly down her throat, but offered no food to spare for the dying woman. She knew faintly that it was daytime.

Yes, she recalled, just that morning she had for some reason been moved to pray. She had never seen a doctor for her sickness, and she did not know if treatment existed. She knew only that death was close. "Lord, if I don't get help, I will die this week. This is the end."

Her eyes quivered at a sound. Was that the sound of a car door? She struggled to sit up and peeked out the window. Outside, a woman was walking toward her door.

"I saw the sun and the sky, and how bright the world is. I stood there and it was like walking in heaven. I kept saying 'It's so beautiful.'"

A stream of light flooded into the room. The sick woman sank back onto the bed as the neglected door scraped across the floor, and in walked the nurse. With a quiet gasp, Jules knelt beside the bed, reached for the wrinkled hands of that jumble of skin and bones, and began to whisper soothing words of prayer. As she asked for God's mercy to save the woman's life, she felt the dehydrated body shaking in tearless sobs.

It was this moment that Charmaine loved retelling most of all. "She prayed for me," she told me. "She didn't do anything else. Just prayed. And promised to come back."

Six months had passed since Jules's first visit when an expat friend introduced me to Charmaine. Her clear and articulate English hid the fact that she had never learned to read or write. For six months she had been visiting the hospital regularly, taking ARV drugs twice every day, and eating healthy vegetables, milk, and occasional meat. She was still thin, but had gained a lot of weight back. She told me little about the healing of her physical body, though. What she spoke about was God and the healing of her soul.

"You know the next day, the day after the nurse came, I woke up and looked at my curtains. I said 'these curtains are so dirty.' And I walked outside. I saw the sun and the sky, and how bright the world is. Honestly, the nurse still had not done anything for me. I had not eaten in a month. But I stood there and it was like walking in heaven. I just saw everything new and I kept saying 'It's so beautiful.'"

From that day on, Charmaine saw life as more beautiful and worth living each day. Jules had visited again and again. One day she brought paint to make bright red and white stripes down Charmaine's door and semicircle shapes around the windows. These had been the first thing I noticed about the house that day. Instead of the house's isolation, I saw these two colorful windows opening to visitors like blooming flowers.

As we talked, Charmaine sat on the edge of her colorful bedspread wearing a red sweater that matched the flowers on the house. Even after six months of steady weight gain, her clothes hung loosely from her shoulders. Her kindly wrinkled face, black polyester slacks, and knit sweater reminded me of my own grandmother, but in fact she was probably younger than my mother.

My expat friend and I sat with knees almost touching a small coffee table between us. The single room contained a bed, couch, chair, stove burner, two small tables, and a countertop plus all her earthly possessions. At first living in this square little hand-built cottage at the edge of the woods struck me as quaint. Later I realized there was something odd about the home: it wasn't the size but the loneliness. Every other Zulu home I had visited was part of a group of buildings. As families grew, instead of building an addition on a house, they added more buildings to a homestead—round ones, square ones, lined up or circled together like friends. I remembered the pieces of Charmaine's story that my friend had told me on our ride there. Charmaine's family had specifically chosen that home for Charmaine to go die in alone. I had heard of the stigma aimed at people with HIV, even known examples like the customers afraid to buy Nikiwe's food because of her sick sister. In some cases, people blamed the sickness on a curse by a neighbor or a punishment from unsatisfied ancestors. In other cases, uninformed Christians regarded the disease as the sick person's punishment from God. This was especially painful for rape victims or people who contracted the disease from an unfaithful spouse. On top of this, old rumors about the disease spreading through personal contact died hard. Whether traditional beliefs, misguided Christianity, or fearful ignorance of the disease were to blame for the ostracism, my heart ached imagining this grandmotherly woman abandoned to die.

Her own mother lived just three houses up the road but still could not admit that Charmaine was HIV positive. "We discussed it once," Charmaine explained to me. "My mother said, 'No, Charmaine, not you. You don't have that disease.' I don't tell her any more. She doesn't want to know."

As she talked, she went to her dresser drawer and took out a wrinkled photograph of a man in his twenties, her nephew. She described her horror when she found him by accident one day, hidden in a back room of her mother's house. Refusing to get tested for HIV, he had come there to die. Charmaine's mother shouted away the local missionary Pabble and a pastor when they came to insist that the young man get treatment. The young man died soon after.

"Have things changed since then?" I asked. "Are people more accepting of the disease now?"

She stared at me for a few seconds and shook her head slowly. "No, I can't say things have changed. You see, even now why would I want to tell people when all they're going to do is laugh and laugh? Some people just like to talk about other people and feel like it makes them better."

Charmaine's family was not sure what to do with her. Her mother visited occasionally but never mentioned the months she had forsaken Charmaine.

Still, Charmaine loved to tell them what she learned about God, and she did not give up hope for them. "I know God changed my life," she told me. Since Jules's visit she had fallen more and more in love with Christ, her body and soul's Savior. "I drank all the time when I was young. I lived a terrible life. I tell you many of the people I knew have died now. Some shot, some sick. But even when I was drunk, I would go in the toilets. And I would pray."

The day I opened Charmaine's door carrying her sewing machine, she sank onto her bed and wept.

She was also praying especially for her son who was serving the last months of a several-year prison term. Much of the little cash she got her hands on went toward cell phone airtime to call him. She dreamed of building a house for him and his children when he returned. Meanwhile the grandchildren's mother spent many evenings out drinking and sleeping around. Often Charmaine would find her grandchildren, ages two and four, locked at home alone.

"God has answered all my prayers so far," she said. "I just wait and know He will answer the next ones too."

She told me her life story without my asking, and by the time I went home I had resolved to return with pen and paper to record the details. The story would become the first of a series of e-mails I sent to friends. Soon I was sending out stories every two weeks, and these stories would form the groundwork for this book.

At the time I visited Charmaine, the nurse had just left for America. Other foreigners and volunteers in the area were picking up where she left off, visiting Charmaine weekly to bring food, read the Bible with her, and spend time playing with her grandchildren who lived nearby. Charmaine had no ID book, which meant she could not receive the government grant available for nonworking sick or retired South Africans. A church's food parcel program provided her a five-pound bag of cornmeal, some sugar, and some cooking oil every month, but for her body to stay strong, she desperately needed the vegetables, milk, and eggs friends were bringing her each week. Meanwhile foreign volunteers and some South African Christian and humanitarian volunteers welcomed her into a multiracial church, provided her part-time work embroidering handbags, celebrated Christmas with her, and taught her to print her name.

Through the network of foreign volunteers, Sofi met Charmaine and began helping her in the long process of applying for an ID book and grant. Charmaine dreamed of the day she would receive her first grant, 750 rand a month, about a hundred U. S. dollars. "I will save until I can buy a sewing machine," she told me. As a young woman she had owned a sewing machine and could sew dresses without patterns, but years ago, her sewing machine had been stolen. Charmaine glowed when she told me how she was praying for a means to start a sewing business, in addition to learning to read and write.

At the time, I had just shared Charmaine's story in an e-mail to some friends. One woman wrote back, "I don't know how I can go on reading these stories without being able to do something to help. Please tell me if you know someone I could give a gift to." I immediately thought of Charmaine's sewing machine. When I imagined the joy with which Charmaine would receive a sewing machine and calculated the months it would take for her to save the money herself, I knew this gift was meant for her.

The day I opened Charmaine's door carrying her sewing machine, she sank onto her bed and wept. Before I could open it, she insisted that we sit on the bed, squeezing each other's hands while she prayed out her thanks to God.

I returned a few days later to check that she had the machine assembled and running. Before she opened the sewing machine case, she slipped behind the bed to a dresser crammed into the corner. With her back to me, she opened a drawer and drew out a tiny booklet, slowly turning the pages and brushing her fingers over them like a holy artifact. Then she turned to me, held out the booklet, and slid her fingers over the letters on a—all in capitals of shakily drawn sticks—CHARMAINE. This was the signature in her long-awaited ID booklet, the key to monthly pension money.

A few months later, Charmaine's son finished his prison term. She was overjoyed to have him living with his children and their mother again, but the celebrating didn't last. Soon he was struggling. He missed a week of work for sickness and lost his job, and a month later his girlfriend had a miscarriage. Charmaine worried herself sick and began losing weight. She talked to her son often about HIV and encouraged him to get tested, but like many South Africans, he came up with reason after reason to put it off.

"It doesn't matter if you're white or black or where you come from. God has given me all of you as my family."

Less than a year after leaving prison, he was caught stealing a lawn mower.

I came to visit her two days after her son was put in jail again. I found her midway down her road, walking the three miles into town to bring her son some food at the jail. I parked my motorcycle at a neighbor's house and joined her as she walked.

"I don't understand," she said. "I pray to God, and why do these things happen to me?" She sounded tired, but not from physical exertion. I thought as she climbed a hill without so much a pause to catch her breath that she was already well past the average South African woman's life expectancy of only forty-eight years.[10]

"It isn't easy being a Christian, is it?" I offered her a smile, but she kept her eyes on the ground. Another car rushed past us, offering a welcome moment for me to think of anything better to say. I kept expecting someone to offer us a ride, but no one did.

"Charmaine," I asked. "How do you stay so hopeful, living with HIV?" I had heard many stories of people sinking into depression when they got their HIV test results, some even committing suicide.

"I just don't focus on the dying part,'" she said. "Some people, when they find out they're HIV positive, that's all they can think about. And thinking about dying, that's what's killing them. I just say, 'I take my ARV medicine, and I'm going to die when God wants me to die.'"

We walked for a while in silence. I took off my sweatshirt and wrapped it around my waist while Charmaine kept a steady pace in front of me.

"You know," she said suddenly, pausing for me to walk beside her. "God knew I needed a family, so He gave me this new family. I have had so many friends from far away visiting me and helping me. It doesn't matter if you're white or black or where you come from. God has given me all of you as my family."

I thought of my own family miles away, the grandmothers my children saw only once a year at most. I reached out to squeeze her hand. "God knew I needed a family, too."

We were halfway to town and I needed to turn back to fetch my motorcycle in time for a meeting. We hugged and parted ways, but after a few minutes I turned around to watch her thin silhouette carrying on into the distance. As my feet crunched the gravel on the side of the road, brushing through weeds and into the grass when cars passed, I remembered the famous advice to walk a mile in someone else's shoes. I had not made it quite a mile walking beside Charmaine, and neither would I ever fully understand how it felt to be HIV positive in a traditional Zulu society. Aid workers and concerned Christians, many who were now her close friends, had improved her life—even saved her life. It remained to be seen how well any of us could provide what she needed in the long run. I heard rumors that an old friend had started pressuring Charmaine toward drinking alcohol, and lately most of her foreign friends had been too busy to visit or had moved away. She had switched to an all-Zulu church, one of the few in the area led by a seminary-trained evangelical pastor. I hoped maybe there someone would offer friendship of the kind Charmaine craved. In the end, hers was a hard road, and she was walking it mostly alone.

Still, every day she got out of bed, straightened the curtains on her blooming-flower windows, swept the floor and yard, fed her chickens, and kept everything as tidy as the day she first opened her windows on a new life.

QUESTIONS *for discussion and reflection:*

1. What is stigma and how does it worsen the effects of HIV/AIDS?

2. If the traditional belief system blames sicknesses on disrespecting ancestors or curses cast by neighbors, how do these beliefs contribute to stigma? How might misdirected Christians also contribute to stigma?

3. Across the world 33 million people, nearly equal to the population of California, are infected with HIV. Of these, 68 percent are in sub-Saharan Africa, and more are in South Africa (5.5 million) than in any other nation.[11] How can the church support people living with HIV/AIDS? How can the church work toward slowing the spread of the disease?

4. What examples does the Bible offer of how Jesus related to people with diseases that held stigma within Jewish culture at the time?

5. Examine your own heart—do you hold any stereotypes about people with HIV/AIDS, sexually transmitted diseases, or other sicknesses? How do you behave when you are around sick people? How do you feel about death?

BEAUTIFUL LANGUAGE:
CORINA

I carefully placed one leg over a clump of lilies into a bed of soft groundcover that wafted a minty smell of leaves crushing under my toes. Corina, whose garden I was trampling, stretched her arm across a prickly bush to hand me a bundle of leaves and dangling roots.

"Take that one, too," she said. "I only know its name in Afrikaans, but whatever you call it, you'll find it's very beautiful."

Corina plunged a shovel into a bed of garlic-scented grass with tiny purple flowers. Her gardener, a man about my age who followed us silently around the garden, took the shovel from her hands and scooped out a basketball-sized clump of roots and soil.

"Maybe that's enough." I wiped my face on my T-shirt sleeve. The midmorning summer sun, even at our mountain-foothill altitude, made an hour of digging feel like enough work for a day. Zeke, about two at this time, and Phoebe tested their strength trying to lift two sacks already full of plants, and as many more lay scattered on the lawn. I had met Corina only twice before, but when I mentioned that I had just hoed up a bed for flowers along the edge of my bare lawn, she invited me to take cuttings and plants from her own garden to get mine started.

Sweat showed at the edges of Corina's light brown hair and there were smudges of dirt across her long purple skirt. "How would you like to come inside for some tea or juice? Phoebe, Zeke, would you like some biscuits?"

They answered with eager nods.

"It's going to take all winter to plant all this, Corina." I laughed as I threw a final cutting onto the pile. I wondered how many South Africans thought I was crazy for breaking up clods of grass with my own blistered hands on a hoe and trying to maintain flower and vegetable gardens in addition to work and family. The thought of hiring someone to sweat through the heat of the day just so that I could have colorful blossoms along my fence line made me cringe, though. Becoming just another boss of underpaid manual laborers seemed to conflict with everything I had come to South Africa to accomplish. Often when I made new acquaintances, I felt like my white face alone sent up a barrier that said to South Africans, as it would in much of the world, "I am your employer, oppressor, object of envy, or donor." Many times I wished I could change that message to say just "friend," but it was not as simple as writing in bold letters on a T-shirt "I am just a human like you," or driving around with a loudspeaker announcing, "You and I are both equally valuable, precious, important, and worthy of dignity because God loves us."

As women of the same race, Corina and I did not have to cross the same layers of misunderstanding, hurt, and guilt that clouded and cluttered friendships with many black South Africans. Still we would not have become friends if not for her generosity and a common interest in beautiful things. She had introduced herself to me in a gift shop one day and explained she had heard I was new in town and might need furniture. "I have a small cabinet you might like," she said in a gentle voice, thick with an Afrikaans accent. "It's not very new, but maybe you could paint it." Her assumption that I would enjoy decorating a cabinet surprised me, but when she dropped off the cabinet and we stood admiring the possibilities of its curved drawers and legs, I felt inspired to match the kindness of her gift with a creative attempt. I dipped into the leftovers of two cans of paint I had used for our walls—yellow and white—to lavish swirling flowers and leaves onto the sides and top of the cabinet.

As I followed Corina inside for tea, the same artistic touches that she displayed in her garden greeted me in every corner. Before joining the housekeeper to prepare the tea, she led us to her daughter's bedroom where the children could play. The bedroom walls and ceiling were painted so realistically with baby-blue and billowing white clouds that she said her own children played a game of finding elephants and clown shapes in the clouds. On the way back to the sitting room, I noticed that nearly everything in the bright and colorful house was adorned with some hand-painted design. Waist-high tins just inside the door had cabbages painted on their lids. The walls were covered in art ranging from children's pastel drawings, to Corina's own paintings of teacups and mountains, to prints of masterpieces from around the world. Half of the sitting room doubled as an art studio. A sketch of flowers lay on one of the large tables behind me, surrounded by jars of paintbrushes and colored pencils. Rust colored cattle stampeded off a canvas propped on an easel in a corner. For Corina, visual art was a medium of communication and an expression of joy.

Beyond the decorated walls, I could see through the window to where the hired gardener was picking up the remaining flowers. He jabbed a pitchfork into the grass and leaned on it for a moment to rest. Another man drove a tractor in the distance. Nearly every white family I knew in South Africa employed at least one domestic worker. Family-sized farms usually hired an additional half-dozen or more farmworkers, compared to the family dairy farm that my husband grew up on, which could never afford to employ anyone besides the mom, dad, and the kids of the family. In a developing country like South Africa where so many people needed work, the competition for jobs drove prices down to the point where I wondered whether it was better to pay someone such pathetic wages or not hire anyone at all. At least once a week, I met someone who would have been happy to work for me. We sometimes paid teenagers to wash our car, and we followed our landlord's suggestion to hire a woman once a week to help with housekeeping and babysitting. We paid a few rands more than the rate we had heard other farmers paid starting domestic workers, but still our price seemed absurd in my U.S. paradigm: $6.50 a day.

"I have met many Zulu women who make beautiful beadwork. When I began to work with Zulu women doing beadwork, I saw we have this language in common."

And aside from the low pay, our relationship of white employer to black employee was far from friendship. Some days I invited our housekeeper to eat with us, but she kept her eyes on the table and returned my attempts at conversation in both Zulu and English with one-word answers. Other times she gave me quizzical smiling headshakes as if she, too, thought I was crazy for creating this norm-shattering scene. I still felt twinges of guilt when I served my children tuna sandwiches and sliced vegetables and she quietly slipped outside to eat her cornmeal porridge, or when I typed at my computer and she swept around my feet without more than a sentence of conversation.

Still, at least she had a job. She would have worked for me more days of the week if I offered, whether or not I ate and conversed with her. I was caught between meeting her immediate needs or following my idealistic notion that hiring a gardener or domestic worker would perpetuate a history of lost dignity among black and economically disadvantaged people. Thus far Corina and I had caught only snatches of conversation between the gardening, but I hoped conversation with her would help sort out my dilemma.

I first saw Corina's insights into South African culture on the second time we crossed paths, when she visited the group of eighteen- to twenty-five-year-olds from a nearby township that I was coaching in leadership and business skills. She had asked the group's leader for time with the students to get their feedback on an art series she was about to enter in a competition.

I joined the eight young people and a handful of Corina's friends in crouching beside Corina's nine framed art pieces propped against a wall. Every frame held a common pattern— one Zulu reed mat, covered with one white cloth serviette, divided into six squares. In each of the six squares was a pattern. Some were embroidered with white, beige, or black thread. Others held traditional Zulu beadwork shapes, neatly attached.

We milled back to our seats and Corina started the discussion. "I wanted to show how AIDS makes me feel," her timid voice quaked as she searched for words. "Through my art, I have met many Zulu women who make beautiful beadwork. When I began to work with Zulu women doing beadwork, I saw we have this language in common. This is how we express ourselves—in art, like my embroidery here and their beadwork here.

"See, this piece is happy." She touched a cloth napkin covered in cheerful colors, neatly checkered with Zulu beads and her own delicate embroidery. "This is how I feel at first as we become friends. But then, see here, there are holes. And I feel like this."

We stared at the napkin in the next frame. Empty white circles took the place of some of the beadwork. Black embroidery scribbled wild circles around the empty holes. In other squares, the embroidery spelled out words.

"These are words I took from a medical textbook on HIV/AIDS. This is how I want to react. I want to just tell them the technical answers. You can get medicine for this. You don't have to die. I want it to be technical like that."

Each frame held a mix of squares, some the technical writing, others the holes, others beadwork in shades of grey. She had sewn a white veil over some squares—both the Zulu beads and the embroidery. "What do you think these veils mean?" she asked the group.

Slowly the words came out from both the blacks and the whites in the room: *These veils are denial. We all do it. We don't want to discuss it. When we're done shouting, we shut up. We don't know how to talk about it.*

One of Corina's friends asked the youth, "Were you surprised to find there's this white woman here in this community, making this artwork and feeling this way?"

A young man let out a puff of breath. "Surprised? Sure! We don't know you feel this too."

Corina led the discussion from frame to frame, talking through the emotions of interacting with people with HIV, ending with colorful, hopeful pieces that expressed her faith that life on earth does not have to be the end for a suffering person. When she finished, I felt she had offered us a message from deeper in her heart than many people share in years of friendship.

I looked forward to hearing more from Corina's heart as she and the housekeeper joined me in her sitting room with a tray of teacups, teapot, juice, and cookies, or biscuits as she called them. The children guzzled their juice and headed outside, cookies in hand.

> *"You must remember, the system kept us apart."*

"Do you mind if I ask," I ventured when our tea was poured, "how did you get interested in Zulu beadwork? I mean, that art you shared with us, I would love to hear more about the relationships that inspired it."

She slowly finished chewing a bite. "I just wasn't exposed to things as a child," she began. "I went to an all-white school, and all-white university. The racial barrier is so strong. It's put into you as a child. I was always taught to be respectful and friendly to farmworkers, but I was never in a situation where I was with someone black who could be a friend."[12]

She explained that her grandparents were Afrikaners, Dutch-descended immigrants who had lived in South Africa for generations. After the Boer War around the turn of the twentieth century, these Afrikaners spread out from the English-controlled South Africa across the continent. Corina's grandfather moved to Tanzania, but her father made his way back to South Africa's mountainous KwaZulu-Natal Province in search of farmland. The farm where Corina and her husband now lived and raised corn, soybeans, and beef cattle was just a few miles from her childhood home.

"It was actually when I finished school and spent some months traveling in Europe that I first began to see things differently." During that time she began reading books banned in her own country that were written about South Africa by South Africans. She also found South African artwork that had never been displayed in South Africa. One afternoon she walked into an art gallery in Sweden and discovered a painting by a South African artist named Sue Williamson. "The painting showed a blonde woman in tribal clothing. Just that. It seemed so strange to me. I burst into tears."

Corina struggled for words to describe the transformation that began during her time in Europe. "I thought, 'This can't all be true.' I had always seen black people on the street and they looked so happy. You must remember, the system kept us apart."

Back in her own country, she took a job as a teacher in an all-white school but kept questions in the back of her mind. One day her domestic worker mentioned to her, "You don't have to pay for schoolbooks, but we have to." She had never known this fact of her country. Whites received books for free in school, blacks paid for theirs. Now every time she handed out books to the pupils in her white-only school, she came face-to-face with the inequalities that had surrounded her all her life.

When apartheid ended in 1994, the legal and political backing to racism ended, but at an interpersonal level, change between whites and blacks happened slowly. She married and settled into farming life with her husband, and together they continued to discuss how their lives could play a part in healing relationships between blacks and whites.

"One day I was throwing away some old paintings," she told me. "My housekeeper picked them up and took them home. The fact that she wanted artwork was something so simple, but it really struck me. I realized she wanted to improve her home. I had never thought what her home looked like. Now suddenly I acknowledged her as a woman who wanted to make her house pretty, too. I saw we shared that."

Around the same time, Corina noticed a trend of ethnic patterns in interior design and saw a potential to incorporate Zulu beadwork into her own art. "You know what white guilt is?" she asked me.

I had heard the term used before to describe philanthropy aimed at black people from the selfish motive of avoiding dealing with one's own privileged status. I had grappled with this issue myself. As we confront the atrocities committed by people in our own nation, race, or culture, we naturally and rightly come to feel that a part of the guilt for those wrongs belongs to ourselves. Then we have two options: to carry that guilt as a motivation for trying to fix everything ourselves; or confess that guilt, release it to Jesus, and act out of the freedom and love that comes from being forgiven.

"I don't want white guilt to be my motivation for anything," Corina went on. "Maybe sometimes it is, and maybe we can never really tell. But this beadwork connection didn't start out of white guilt. It started because I was interested in their craft."

Beadwork has always played an important role in Zulu culture. At traditional weddings, brides wear elaborate designs sometimes with entire skirts covered in beads, plus beaded anklets, bracelets, necklaces, and belts. There are specific designs to convey meaning for many situations, from coming-of-age ceremonies to family lineage, to messages between lovers.

"I wanted to learn more about their designs. I would find women in town wearing traditional beadwork and tell them to meet back at a certain date to sell things to me. They would promise to come, but then never arrive.

"We're threatening to them, I suppose," Corina continued. "I think white people are vilified in a way."

Seeing Corina's hands gently cradling her teacup and hearing her soft motherly voice, I could hardly imagine her being anything like a villain. I knew that unless others could know her as more than a face, though, there was no difference between her and others who committed atrocities in her nation.

"I'm sure it isn't easy for them to approach us either," she continued. I recalled how my attempts at friendship with our housekeeper, as challenging as they were for me, seemed to make the housekeeper even less comfortable.

Phoebe and Zeke ran inside, shouting that they had found the wading pool and it was a hot day and could they swim. Corina's daughter, several years older than Phoebe, agreed to watch them. Ten minutes later they were stripped to their underwear squealing happily in the waist-deep water.

"So then one day this woman just arrived at my door wearing traditional beaded clothing and offering to sell," Corina continued after the interruption. "Ngoneni was her name. She was so cheeky and confident. We started to have a very fun relationship. We were both just curious about each other. I started learning beading terminology, and she would ask about the pictures on my computer. Everyone else was afraid to even come to my door, or at least they would wait at the gate. But some days I would just turn around and discover Ngoneni had walked in and was sitting on my sofa! She was never in a submissive position to me."

"Art is such a cross-cultural thing. We're artificially separated, and we need these vehicles to take away the threat so we can communicate."

"That kind of relationship is hard to find," I said, then shared my struggle of wanting to share friendship and dignity with our housekeeper even as I offered her the kind of work that could so easily slide toward feeling demeaning. "It's like the only relationships you can have across cultures here are employee-employer or recipient-donor."

"It's difficult, isn't it," Corina spoke slowly. We were both digging for truth as we talked. "Even with Ngoneni, sometimes I felt it wasn't a normal friendship. First of all there was always the language barrier. I learned beading terminology, but we couldn't really talk about feelings—things like HIV or whether her husband loved her or what art meant to us. And there were times she would ask me for money or help typing her CV, and I wondered if she was using me for access to material things. But she did give back to me, too. She loved giving me seeds from her garden, indigenous varieties my husband wanted to learn about. And what she gave me most of all was access to her culture."

Over time Ngoneni began inviting other beading women to Corina's home on appointed dates. "She opened a door to a flood of people," Corina said. "I started building relationships with those women, too. It was some of them, plus employees I have known over the years, who I watched getting sick from HIV. That's why I made those pieces you saw.

"Art is such a cross-cultural thing," she said. "We're artificially separated, and we need these vehicles to take away the threat so we can communicate. Even now, when I run into some of those young people who saw those art pieces, we can start a conversation now."

Much of Corina's artwork expresses this concept directly. She opened a trunk and showed me a piece whose Afrikaans title translates *What We Learned from Our Grandmothers*. In the wall hanging she had blended together European-style crocheted lace that she learned to make from her grandmother with Ngoneni's Zulu beadwork in similar patterns. In

another piece, called *Loveletters*, Corina mixed Zulu "love letters"—bead pieces whose colors and designs would have con-
veyed messages of the depth of love between Ngoneni and
her husband while they courted—with embroidered replicas
of the letters Corina exchanged with a boyfriend in the army
years ago. Studying each piece was like reading a series of messages that promised reconciliation was possible.

"I sometimes ask myself," she continued, "why God made
me an artist. You know, back in Europe before many people
were literate, art was an important Christian vocation. I would
have been making stained glass
windows or painting church ceil-
ings because the church needed
artists to communicate ideas and
stories with illiterate people.
Then I wouldn't have wondered
why I'm an artist.

*"It's hard to know
whether you'll be
more effective in your
own culture or
another. There are
never any recipes
with God."*

"Now I see that as an artist
I've learned to communicate
things visually, like how I feel
about HIV, how I feel living in
this culture and this country,
things I could not explain otherwise. I believe beauty touches
you to an extent where you're willing to open yourself to
God."

"It's like a language you can speak with any culture," I
interjected.

"Yes, but it's just one way. I think we South Africans need
to share other ideas on how to overcome racism. There must
be more ways to change the way we relate across cultures.
Maybe my friends have ideas I could learn from, but we need
to talk about these issues."

"South Africans aren't the only ones," I told her. "I think

the questions you face here in South Africa are no different than what people anywhere in developed countries need to face. Most people where I come from earn the same kind of income as you or more, and most of our churches are just as racially divided as yours here. Americans and Europeans might not live right next door to as many unemployed people as here in South Africa, but technology and plane tickets and highways leave us with no excuse not to know they are there. We need more people like you finding creative ways to cross cultures."

Already I was scheming of how I could invite a certain woman I had been meaning to visit to come help me plant my sacks of plants. She lived near us and her son of about Phoebe's age had come to play at our house. Once when I had passed her house, I had commented on her orderly rows of cabbages, spinach, and carrots, and the several peach trees around the garden fence. She had offered to give me a peach seedling, but we had not met again since. I suspected she would appreciate the extra income of a day or two of labor, but I was determined to also use the gardening as a communication pathway the way Corina had used art. I was going to be hoeing and digging in the garden anyway; if I invited her to join me, the work would at least open a time for our children to play as equals and offer the possibility of a friendship based on our common interest in gardening.

"There are so many questions to consider," Corina said. "Even now, my husband and I are talking about starting to attend the African church in town."

I had never met a South African of British or Afrikaans descent who considered immersing themselves as a member of an all-black church. My husband and I attended a Zulu church where many American volunteers visited from time to time, but I knew it was easier for us to break stereotypes because we were already outsiders. There were challenges to sitting through the long services that our children didn't understand, and occasional awkwardness around people who must have wondered why we didn't go to church with our own race like everyone else. We loved learning from the pastor's insights into Christianity in the context of his culture, though, and among the people we sat beside each week, some had become real friends.

"We're finding it difficult to decide where God wants us," she said. "I can also stay where I am at the Dutch Reformed Church," a church that held services in Afrikaans. "We see being there as another way of changing things, kind of like the parable of the yeast that spreads through the whole dough little by little. It's hard to know whether you'll be more effective in your own culture or another. It's not always a decision you can make in a rational way. There are never any recipes with God."

The more I heard from Corina, the more I recognized the false assumptions that I brought to South Africa—namely, that white South Africans were heartless racists. How could people live next door to people in extreme poverty and do nothing to help? Sure, I was descended from people who did as much and worse to Native Americans and slaves, but surely this was different. I didn't have Native Americans working in the hot sun hoeing my garden, or serving me tea and cake in my parlor. I didn't live in a four-bedroom home in a country where the richest 10 percent of the population owned more than 44 percent of the wealth.[13] And yet I did come from one of the most powerful countries in the world with plenty of its own faults, and I lived in the same world that on a whole spread wealth even more unequally than South Africa. I faced the same responsibility as my white South African friends to confess, forgive and be forgiven, and walk humbly and justly in the response to our enormous inheritance of guilt.

It was nearing lunchtime. I called the children inside and helped them pull their clothes back on while we wrapped up conversation, then said good-bye some more as we walked to my car.

The gardener met us at the car with the sacks of plants and loaded them into the car trunk. When he finished, I carefully smiled and looked him in the eye as I thanked him in Zulu. He looked down without replying. For him looking at the ground was a gesture of respect, I knew. More than ever, though, I was thankful for people like Corina and Ngoneni innovating new languages to give and receive respect as equals.

QUESTIONS *for discussion and reflection:*

1. What is the difference between giving a donation and pursuing a friendship? Describe what is different in the minds and hearts of both the giver and the receiver.

2. Compare Corina to the farmer by Phakamile's home, who said, "They built that fence, not me."

3. Do you think it is easier for a local like Corina or an outsider like the author to make a difference in a country? What are the challenges and advantages of each?

4. What advantages or disadvantages do you have in life because of the place, nationality, race, gender, family, and economic setting you were born into? How does that affect how others view you?

5. Besides art, what other creative methods can you think of to communicate and make friendships between peers across cultures and economic levels? Do you have gifts or interests—such as gardening for the author—that could lead to bridges across cultures in your own country or elsewhere?

DISTANT VOICES:
SABELO

One spring morning I jogged up my driveway, over a bridge, and around a turn, following signs that promised a primary school along that side road. I had moved to the rural neighborhood a few weeks earlier, and when I saw the signs for a school, I imagined the convenience of having Phoebe attend kindergarten the following year within walking distance.

What I found was a cracked signboard labeled "Glen Isla School" with several letters faded away, wired onto a rusted fence. As I peeked through the holes of the fence, I saw a school worse than any I had seen in the country. Weeds grew three feet up the walls, several doors had fallen off, and broken glass littered the ground. Termites had eaten gaping holes into the walls of a fiberboard classroom. The packed-mud exterior of another building was crumbling away, revealing the framework of poles and sticks beneath. Still disbelieving that children learned in this environment, I strained to hear voices to see if this was in fact an active school. Over the clicking of insects in the tall grass and the grumble of a far-off tractor, I could just make out the voices of children reciting multiplication tables and the tapping of a teacher's stick on a chalkboard as he lectured in Zulu.

I closed my eyes. I had seen the children of farm laborers in the neighborhood, some hardly taller than four-year-old

Phoebe, walking over a mile down my road each morning where no school buses ran, and this is what they came to. I let my prayers for those children, their teachers, and this building drift into the heavens amidst the sounds of the voices beyond the fence.

Little did I know, those prayers were part of a long chain of prayers that had been prayed for that school. Over a generation ago, white Christian farmers saw that the children of the farm laborers living around their property were too far from town to attend the nearest public school for blacks under the apartheid system. Believing these children deserved quality schooling, the farm owners erected buildings, hired teachers, and managed a school that became known for providing some of the best education for rural blacks in the area.

About twenty-five years ago, a boy walked the two kilometers from his home to that school building, holding the hand of his older brother, and introduced himself to the headmaster as Sabelo. His mother had been unable to come. She spent each morning cooking huge pots of pap[14] and beans and delivering the food across the fields for the farm laborers, earning a monthly income equivalent to about one hundred U.S. dollars. Each evening she returned home to run a household for nine children, buying them school uniforms and pencils and insisting that they make it to school every day. Sabelo's father had two other wives and disappeared from Sabelo's life when he was just a baby. The single mom did her best to teach how a man should behave. "Please my sons," she told them, "don't drink. Don't smoke. Be good to your wives." And she prayed over them.

When he graduated, Sabelo went on to earn a two-year degree in marketing but could not find a job. He spent two disheartening years searching for work, then decided he might as well visit Glen Isla School, offer his résumé, explain that he had no teaching certification or experience, and see what happened.

The principal glanced through the résumé, pointed to an open door behind him, and said, "There's your classroom. Go teach."

The school had changed drastically since Sabelo attended. When apartheid ended, the government encouraged many privately owned "farm schools" like Glen Isla to become public schools. The theory behind the switches was probably that the schools gained freedom from the hands of white founders. In reality, it would take years to complete paperwork to prove the school property did not belong to the farmers, and the Department of Education was too swamped with upgrading thousands of abysmal-quality rural schools to help much in training or hiring new educators to take over what the farmers had begun.

"Can you imagine what it does to a student's confidence to attend a school like this every day? It's a disgrace."

Sabelo had taught at Glen Isla for a year when I jogged up the road and stood outside the fence hearing his voice mingle with the others in the school. A few months later, I worked up the courage to go inside that fence.

"You can call me Sabelo," the young man said, introducing himself. He taught English and several other subjects for grades seven to nine, the top grades offered at the school.

I had come to Glen Isla with the idea of offering to teach English one morning a week, hoping at the same time I would get to know the teachers and find further ideas of what could be done to improve the school. Soon after I pulled my car through the gate, the principal stepped out of a classroom wiping chalk dust from his hand and extended it into a hand-shake. "Yes please, anything you can offer," he said in a soft voice. "Please, we are so grateful." Then he returned to the classroom he had taught since the latest teacher moved on to a better-paying city job. I returned home to prepare and pray for my first class.

Each Tuesday morning, Phoebe and Zeke played with five other children in the kindergarten/preschool room as I moved from classroom to classroom. First, I would visit the classroom where one teacher taught about thirty students in first through third grades, then another room that covered fourth, fifth, and sixth grades, and then finish the morning with Sabelo's seventh, eighth, and ninth graders. After class I would often talk with the teachers and principal about what the school needed.

Sabelo suggested that we ask children in the United States to donate books for a library. That request would later blossom into several schools raising money and writing letters to the students.

"Repairs are the most desperate need," Andres, the princi-pal, said. "When it rains, the drips come through the roof. The Department of Education doesn't send us anything. Two years ago I requested chairs, and I have written again ever since, ask-ing for many things—windows, ceiling, floors. They send noth-ing. Can you imagine what it does to a student's confidence to attend a school like this every day? It's a disgrace."

I tried to imagine. In six months Phoebe would be old enough to begin the first of the two years of kindergarten that most South Africa children attended. Her options were to walk to this school with some of the neighbors or have me drive her fifteen minutes into town. The school in town had previously been the all-white school, but now technically was open to all students. The only problem was, they would need money for the tightly packed pickup truck or minivan "taxis" to get there, money for the higher school fees (about fifty dollars a month), and good enough English to keep up. Nearly every white child in the area attended, except for a handful of homeschooling families. The quality of that school was not much different from a U.S. school, with certified teachers who spoke English as a first language, colorfully decorated classrooms, and a new computer lab.

I was angered by the thought that my children could so easily attend the school in town, but none of the children at Glen Isla could. The only minibuses that ran along our street were usually packed with adults and too pricey for these poorer families to pay daily. Volunteering at the school and bringing my children to learn a little Zulu in the preschool room one day a week while homeschooling them the other four days seemed the best option, at least for that year.

It was difficult to see any evidence that my teaching helped the students, though. The first through third graders were smiley and energetic, the fourth through sixth graders were attentive learners, and a few of them were downright good at English, but I had all but given up on the seventh through ninth graders. In the classrooms I saw textbooks in English that were far beyond their comprehension level. Their blackboards were full of English words describing parts of the heart, cumulus and nimbus clouds, or how to run a business, but the students could not answer questions as simple as "does your family raise any animals?" or "what subjects do you study in school?"

Often I assigned homework to the older students and found that only a handful had completed it, most of these having rushed through it that morning or blatantly copied each other's work. I had no authority to give them grades, and they knew it.

One week I called on a ninth grade student to read a word on the chalkboard, and she flat out refused. She stood beside her chair completely mute, staring down at the pen she twirled between her fingers. I asked the rest of the class if someone could help her. No one said a word. Some boys in the back row snickered. I could feel my cheeks turning red as the silence stretched longer. I grabbed the pen out of the girl's hands. All eyes snapped to attention as if I were about to prove my authority with some act of violence or cleverness, but I had none. I told her to sit down, mentally scrapped the rest of my plans for the class, and finished class early without asking any more questions.

"I'm sorry for that." Sabelo approached me as I was tying on Zeke's shoes after class. I had hoped to slip out without speaking to anyone. Already I was considering how to gently break the news that I would not be teaching his class anymore unless I saw some improvement in the students' participation.

I could not fathom how people who lived in such shortage and disappointment day after day managed.

"I tell them the same things you tell them," he shook his head. "I tell them again and again simple things like how to write periods after sentences and how to use 'is' and 'be' correctly. But they never do."

"What do you think they'll do after they finish here?" I stood and faced him. The students were filing out of the classroom and past the big shade tree where my car and the principal's were parked, in the direction of a spindly volleyball net stretched across a field.

"Many of them won't finish. They drop out in grade eight, sometimes nine. Some have babies. Even if they finish grade nine, most of them don't have the money for taxis[15] to continue at the high school in town."

Phoebe came out of the preschool room carrying a paper decorated with glued-on sticks and sprinkled with glitter that had been donated from overseas.

"They don't learn because they don't care," he went on. "School has no use for them. I tell them I was in this very same school, and look at me now, with a degree and a job. But they go work on farms because they want to earn money now . . . or they need to. Many of them don't have parents and their families need the money. HIV is really hitting this place hard. The girls who have babies, maybe it's because they know they get a government grant for a child. They don't understand that someday they will want to have an education so they can earn more than what they earn on a farm.

"But it's funny," he added, letting out a nervous chuckle as his face squeezed into an awkward smile. "I have worked here for a year now. But I have never been paid."

I jerked my head away from watching the student volleyball game to stare at him in amazement. "What?"

His eyebrows rose slightly as he shrugged. "I have never been paid," he repeated.

"What? Why? I mean—"

"There is some kind of mix-up with the papers."

"Is anyone getting paid?"

"Yes. It's just me and one other teacher not getting paid."

"How do you survive? What do you live on?"

"My brothers are working."

I could not fathom how people who lived in such shortage and disappointment day after day managed. I found it infuriating just to come once a week and see no progress in the students, much less spend a year working full-time there with no proof that pay would ever come.

At the same time, I was working with the principal, Andres, toward improving the school building. During a visit to the United States, I had received on behalf of the school about three thousand dollars in donations plus two heavy sacks of children's books to start a library. The donations came from schoolchildren, Sunday schools, friends, and strangers. We hoped to use the money for renovations of the buildings, but three thousand dollars would not even cover the cost of rebuilding one classroom. Before we spent any money, the school board and I agreed we should press more on the South African Department of Education to play their overdue part in the repairs. Andres and I also started a phone-calling campaign to the electric company, urging them to come install the few wires it would take to bring electricity from the neighboring dairy farm into the school. Several of the donating groups continued sending letters to the school and e-mails to me, asking how they could pray. I appreciated their prayers more each day as the building project sat waiting in the same status as Sabelo's wages.

One week I received an e-mail intended to pass along to Glen Isla's older students, from a high school class in the United States. The younger grades had exchanged a few letters with overseas schools, but this would be the first time I tried to get the high school students to communicate with students overseas.

I made up my mind that I would spend the entire class period ignoring whether or not the students made any attempt to speak English. I brought my laptop computer with a charged battery, sat down at a desk in the middle of the classroom, and began to read questions from the high school students on the other side of the world.

"What subjects do you study in school? Have you seen snow? What sports do you play?" The students answered, slowly drawing out English sentences like teaching a cat to heel on command. Mostly they would hold whispered Zulu discussions by twos or threes, scramble and write notes on their hands or on scraps of paper, shove the paper into someone else's hands, read with a scrunched up face, pause in the middle to ask a neighbor to decipher the note on the hand, then stop and ask Sabelo to translate.

We were sitting at the same height—me in a chair next to them, crowded around a single table to see my computer. Some guys in the back sat on tables, enjoying the casual privilege of resting their black shoes on each other's desks. I insisted they stay seated instead of rising formally when they gave me their answers, but each new speaker still rose at least halfway by habit.

When I thought the e-mail was complete, I asked as an afterthought, "Do you have any questions for the Americans?" Again the frantic whisper conferences and then questions began to pour out. "How much does it cost to attend your schools? Do you have witches in America? Is there still racism in America? We heard of Alabama. Is it racist there? I hear people there are prejudiced against Mexicans. Why is that? Do you like Puff Daddy?"

Some of the questions were for me to answer, others they wanted written to the students. We talked long past the bell that dismissed them for morning break.

After that I came each week and sat at one of their desks with questions about their lives and topics to discuss about my own life. One week an American high school teacher visited and made a video of their class, complete with a song sung by Sabelo and a backup choir of students.

Sabelo shared stories from his own childhood, and I learned that he had always been one of the shortest students in the school, too short to play volleyball or soccer, so he took up jogging down the same road I had jogged to first discover Glen Isla. He also shared with a smile that he had attended a colored high school. Under apartheid, "coloreds," or people of lighter skin tones than blacks due to mixed racial heritage or foreign descent, received slightly less discrimination and better public services than black people. Sabelo, seeing the possibility of better education and knowing that his skin was lighter than the average black person, showed up at the colored school and gave a false last name, a name South Africans would recognize as colored, not Zulu. It worked. He was accepted into the colored school and spent the next five years enjoying the highest quality education in the area for a person of his skin tone. Sabelo's English teacher led class discussions that spurred critical thinking and assigned books and poetry that portrayed interracial friendships. Years later, Sabelo was incorporating the same literature into his own teaching.

And then one morning, half a year after I began teaching at Glen Isla, Adam and I received an e-mail welcoming us to teach development courses at a seminary in a city one and a half hours away. The position was a perfect match of our skills and the seminary's needs, and within two visits to the seminary, we knew God was leading us there. As we drove home from the second visit to the seminary, I stared out the window at the grass-roofed houses scattered across the hillsides and the children walking home from school in their uniforms and backpacks. My heart ached at the thought of tearing out roots that had only just begun to grow. Of all the projects we would have to wrap up and pass into other hands, working with Glen Isla felt the least complete.

What I had accomplished there seemed pathetic compared to the needs. I had brought a donation of children's books, but I suspected the teachers were so worried about wrecking them that students rarely touched them. I had taught them some English, but probably not enough to make a difference in finding a job or reading a textbook. As for chances of any spiritual change as a result of my visits, I couldn't predict anything. And the three thousand dollars sat in my bank gathering dust. It was a waiting game, hoping we could spend it elsewhere instead of draining it into fixing just floors, roofs, or windows, when the entire class-room might be replaced, as it de-served, by the government.

"I came," I began slowly in my clearest English. "Because I believed that God hears the prayers of African people."

From the first day I stood out-side praying for the school, I had wanted a nicely rounded story of rebuilding the school from the inside out, of joining hands across the world to triumph over difficulties. I had imagined sending home letters about Glen Isla full of hope, success, and gratitude to motivate donors and prayers across the developed world. No one, I as-sumed, would want to hear what a slow process it could be to make a garden out of a desert. It was easier to go on pro-claiming that God's love meant God would fix it now, and that if we prayed hard enough and worked hard enough, re-wards would follow us in predictable regularity.

That story was looking ever more unlikely.

Instead I had found myself wrapped up in the long his-tory of people dedicating themselves to unfinished stories—stories of people groups who do not have the Bible in their language, countries that close their borders to missionaries, this and that prayer request that has been prayed for years or generations. I had lived for over a year just up the road from Glen Isla and felt I hardly accomplished anything. Now from a distance, what chance did I have of helping? Moving away hit like a dropkick to any remaining faith I had that anything would ever improve for Glen Isla.

A few weeks before my final week at Glen Isla, I was packing up papers after meeting with Sabelo's class when I heard one of the young men in the back say something. It sounded like a question in English, but it was too mumbled to understand. Everyone around him laughed, which I had noticed was what usually happened when this particular student talked. This time he seemed annoyed at their laughing, as if what he had asked was extremely serious.

I asked him to repeat it, but now he was retreating into the usual it's-not-cool-to-speak-English shell. "Can you tell me what he said?" I asked the teacher.

"He asked why you are here," Sabelo said, and the room went silent.

I paused. I knew this moment mattered as much or more than any teaching I had done at the school. All eyes were pinned on me, ready to catch every syllable.

"I came," I began slowly in my clearest English, "because I believed that God hears the prayers of African people. I believed God wanted to use me to answer some of those prayers. And I believed that when I couldn't help with an answer to those prayers, I could join in praying."

Sabelo translated. They waited for more. "I saw this place." I looked up at the ceiling collapsing in the corner of the room. "And I knew it wasn't right. I didn't think you would choose to go to a school like this if you could choose. That made me sad. And I believed God was sad about that, too. So I'm doing what I can to help. And I believe that God is helping, too."

The teacher translated again, and then we were all silent. I smiled weakly and picked up my purse. From the back of the room, I heard another mumble. This time no one laughed.

No one stared at their desk; no one twirled a pencil. I looked from face-to-face and read agreement across the room. "What did he say?" I turned to Sabelo again for a translation.

"They say they are grateful."

* * *

When I left Glen Isla, I went on praying, and I e-mailed people in my home continent who also went on praying with probably more faith than I had. Nine months and several dozen phone calls later, the Department of Education had only moved far enough to sign a few papers. Nothing new showed at the school.

Then one day while I sat in the seminary office building preparing to teach a class, I received a phone call from Andres, the principal of Glen Isla School. He said that a few weeks earlier the Department of Education had suddenly arrived at Glen Isla with a computer for his office and an engineer to make plans for renovations. He added that he had enrolled all the teachers in university courses to raise their certification level. And best of all, the Department of Education had returned just that week with a temporary mobile trailer-style classroom. The school board was ready to begin spending our three thousand dollars. They suggested starting with a photocopier (so that teachers would not have to pay for copies themselves in town), a TV/DVD player, a generator (the electric company had lost the school's order number and expected

I knew there was more still to ask God for on behalf of Glen Isla School, but for now, all I needed to say was thank you.

181

another long delay), and burglar bars and a new office door to keep their new purchases safe.

"You opened the door for us," he said. "We feel so blessed."

I hung up the phone, went into the bathroom stall of the office building, locked the door, leaned back against the cool brick wall, and tipped my face toward the ceiling. My hands were shaking and tears slid down my cheeks. I knew there was more still to ask God for on behalf of Glen Isla School, but for now, all I needed to say was thank you.

One year after I left Glen Isla School, I went outside early one morning to empty our trash in the bin. I glanced up at the first rays of sunlight illuminating the steep mountain slope that rose behind the apartment building where we were staying. From somewhere my eyes couldn't quite focus, between the boulders and bushes of the bare landscape, I could just hear the faint sound of voices. They sang with a simple rhythm and a melody that bent and repeated with a kind of longing like a mother separated from her child. As I listened I remembered what a friend had told me—that a group of Christians from the Democratic Republic of Congo, refugees who had fled their war-torn homeland, gathered on that mountain to pray. I wondered whether the singers had climbed the mountain in darkness before dawn or stayed there all night praying and pleading for their homeland and the people they left behind. From thousands of miles away, they were doing what they could on behalf of families, friends, and people they would never meet, people left behind in a war that at the time of their prayers had no end in sight.

I stood in the chill morning air listening to the music, and my thoughts returned to Sabelo. A month earlier he had sent me a short phone message: "I got paid today!" When I called him, his voice was exuberant.

"And will you stay at Glen Isla?" I asked, knowing the lump of pay he received would be enough to cover several months of job searching or the start of another degree.

"I will," he said soberly. "You know, life is not easy, and you have to persevere. You need to have love for what you do. And I do love this place."

"So what will you do with the money?" I asked.

"I bought myself a new pair of shoes!" He laughed. I closed my eyes and recalled the day I spotted him and another teacher walking the last stretch to the school, having taken a minibus and hitchhiked the previous fifteen miles of road. It had been the rainy season and they walked in their bare feet, carrying their shoes. "Mine were in terrible condition from that road." He added that he would set aside the rest to save for a car to drive himself and other teachers to and from school.

Now as I stood looking up at the mountain, I marveled that he had made it through the twenty-five months he had worked without pay and still chosen to stay. Across the world there were many more people like him waiting—some waiting with faith in God, others waiting without much faith at all—but either way they were waiting in impossible situations that only God could solve.

But they were not alone.

Above and around Sabelo, past Glen Isla's rusted fence and beyond his hearing, floated distant voices. Around the world, people undaunted by unfinished stories were joining the chorus, lifting their voices to God on behalf of him and the thousands and millions more Glen Islas and Sabelos who are still waiting.

QUESTIONS *for discussion and reflection:*

1. What experiences have you had of being separated from people you cared for or wanted to help? How did you respond?

2. Read Ephesians 6:18:

   Pray in the Spirit on all occasions with all kinds of prayers and requests. With this in mind, be alert and always keep on praying for all the saints.

   Why do you think Paul reminds and urges Christians to pray? (Read the rest of Ephesians chapter 6 for additional ideas on *how* to pray.)

3. Is there a point at which it is better to give up trying to help a community or an individual? How do you determine when that point is?

4. What would you do if you were responsible for improving the quality of Glen Isla School?

5. How do we know that in the end of all things there is a good final ending to the story of the universe? How does that give us hope for the present?

6. What apparently hopeless unfinished stories do you see in your community or world? In which of these would you like to be involved, through prayer and/or in other ways?

REMEMBER US

"Lord, Your love encompasses the oceans . . ." I sang, feeling the rumbling waves swallow my words. I rested my back against a palm tree and let the wind brush the tears across my cheeks, not caring if my voice drifted far enough for strangers to hear. All day I had felt anonymous, rejected, or at best invisible. Let me go on acting invisible.

I had come to Durban alone. The city of two-and-a-half million people is perhaps most known for beaches, Indian food, and crime. I rode our motorcycle the whole hair-raising two-hour trip down the superhighway to the city and then checked into my hostel (actually *backpacker* is the South African term), only to find I was one of just two females. The rest of the dozen or more visitors were surfers, mostly foreigners, who hovered around the television all night watching surfer movies, surfer contests, and surfer interviews.

I did not come to surf. I was attending a conference two blocks away in the International Convention Centre, a huge state-of-the-art building designed to host events like the recent Miss India Worldwide competition and visits from the likes of former UN Secretary-General Kofi Annan. The conference I attended was sponsored by a government-funded organization that promoted youth entrepreneurship, and more than three hundred delegates attended. Weeks before the conference, I checked prices on all the accommodations recommended for visitors, and hoping to honor a lower budget for our little non-profit, I decided I could handle a backpacker for a couple of nights.

Two days before I left for the convention, as I rode in a car with a young white woman from the farm down the road from ours, I happened to mention the trip. She gripped the steering wheel tighter and got very quiet. "Chrissy, that's a very dangerous neighborhood." She sounded terrified. A few weeks earlier, she had told me a story about a church in Durban that was held up at gunpoint only minutes before she arrived to visit. "Let me get you the names of some other places to stay," she insisted.

Crime in South Africa is a real force to be reckoned with. In 2007 you were twenty times more likely to be murdered by gunshot in South Africa than in the United States.[16] Durban residents frequently awoke to find stoplights nonfunctional because of stolen wiring or water off because of stolen copper pipes. A friend who volunteered with the Peace Corps caught a stray shot from a pellet gun into her stomach while walking in broad daylight in Durban. When our family visited a beach in Durban, Adam felt the swish of a pickpocket's hand reaching into a backpack slung over his shoulder. He spun around, gripped the boy's head in his hand, and growled in his face, "Don't. Do. That." The boy twisted his head free just as Adam noticed his cell phone in the boy's hand. Adam threw down his bag and tore after the boy, drawing the attention of a security guard who caught the boy by the arm. As they waited for a police report, Adam looked the boy in the eye and said, "Look, I forgive you for this. And you might get away from the police this time, or lots of other times, but it doesn't matter what the police say or what I say. What matters is that God sees what you're doing. And if you don't start following Jesus and letting Him turn your life around, you're going to be in an even bigger heap of trouble. Forever."

This kind of apprehension or reconciliation was rare. Usually crime fueled only racism and fear. Durban suburbs offered gated communities with security guards and massive double barriers of electric razor wire fence. Sofi, on the other hand, lived on an isolated farm with neither burglar bars nor fences. Her home was broken into eight times in a single year. Among her losses were a generator, a horse, a set of solar panels, and then a second and third replacement for those solar panels.

When in our Bible study we read Jesus' words, "Love your enemies, do good to those who hate you" (Luke 6:27), Sofi grabbed a box of tissues, laid her head on the table, and sobbed.

"It's just so hard, isn't it?" she said with a giant sniffle. "Every time the dogs bark, I jump out of bed. I'm not getting any sleep."

An American volunteer reached for Sofi's hand. "I used to think if I was being robbed, I would have the faith to flip on the lights and just surprise them with my perfect, calm love— maybe offer them a cup of tea. Now I think more likely I'd just scream and throw things at them. This whole love your enemy thing, it's crazy."

Maybe it was stubbornness, maybe foolishness, maybe a false illusion of safety, or maybe the Holy Spirit leading, but I decided to stick with the backpacker. I thanked my friend for her help, and never told her what I decided.

"I don't understand why you Americans come here. What do you do? Just drive around in your four-wheel-drive vehicle and hand out things and feel good about yourself?"

It wasn't the backpacker full of surfers, rumored to have a brothel on the next floor up, that bothered me. Nor was it the two block walk to the convention center each morning past garages and littered boulevards. It was the loneliness of attending a conference of some three hundred people who seemed to ignore me.

This must be how it feels to be a minority, I thought on the second day of the conference as I sat down with my loaded plate of buffet food. No one at the table acknowledged my presence, and two women stood up to leave. I had noticed only about five other white people at the whole conference, but I wasn't about to give in and go sit with them.

I made up my mind not to be bothered. Making eye contact with strangers is not a cultural norm here, so I tried chalking it up to my own false expectations. Everywhere I went all that morning, I had smiled and greeted people. Most dropped the conversation, but some responded politely enough when I tried to pick their brains on microenterprise and the youth of South Africa. By the end of lunch, I had struck up a conversation with a young Indian man in a beret. As he gathered his things to leave, a young black man wearing a business suit interrupted us.

"So are you one of those people who come here because you think you're going to save us?"

For the next thirty minutes, he hammered me with questions. "I don't understand why you Americans come here," he said. "What do you do? Just drive around in your four-wheel-drive vehicle and hand out things and feel good about yourself?"

I took a deep breath and prayed for humility as my mind scrambled for clear examples. I started by telling him how Adam and I lived in a Nicaraguan village for a year in the deepest poverty we could enter. We ate beans and tortillas for every single meal, washed clothes on rocks, and went without electricity or medical insurance. I told him I would give anything to live like that in South Africa, but could not imagine how. I told him about the black teacher whom we had asked about moving into his neighborhood. The teacher had eyed us soberly and said, "A boy died here last night. No one knows why. You have children. Don't do it."

By now nearly everyone had finished eating and left their tables. "So where are you living now?" the man pressed the subject further.

As if in apology, I explained that we finally decided to rent from a white landlord on a farm with a safe reputation. "That doesn't mean we don't care, though." I wondered if he believed me, or if I even believed myself.

The conversation drifted into other subjects. He showed me pictures of his wife and child and told me about his business as a technology consultant. We ended up parting on terms something like friendship, but it was exhausting. And the thought kept haunting me, *Is this what everybody else thinks of me, too? A white know-it-all who's got no right to intrude?*

I stood on the shore, leaning against the palm tree and singing. "Lord, Your love is deeper than the sea . . ."

Following some reckless impulse, I went for a walk toward the Indian Ocean ten blocks from the conference center. I knew the sun would set soon, and my walk led through what my white friend would definitely deem some dangerous blocks. But I wasn't in a mood to care. I carried no money— only my cheap cell phone in one hand and a set of keys in the other. *Lord,* I prayed, *I just want someone to recognize that we're*

all just human. I want You to show me You love me. And I want
to see how much You love all these people, too.

I watched Zulu women carrying their groceries home,
their wide ankles beneath pinafore dresses identical to those
of my Zulu friends in the countryside, the same scarves
around their heads. Yes, I did love these people. But why was
it so difficult to show them? Why did I feel so unloved? Was
my presence in South Africa just interfering, pretending that
I could do a job they could do well enough on their own?
Would they all be better off if I just went back to my race and
my country?

Ten minutes later I stood on the shore, leaning against the
palm tree and singing. "Lord, Your love is deeper than the sea
. . ." I tried to imagine myself like a tiny speck of sand tumbling
in those waves as if all the ocean were God and His love and
power. The sun dropped below the horizon, and I knew I
should hurry home. Maybe those waves of a vast love were
the best answers I would get. Already it was dark as I chugged
up the last two blocks to the backpacker, past an empty lot
drenched in shadows.

Behind me I heard the voices of two young men. They
were deep in conversation, a curious mix of street Zulu and
English that sounded something like a heated philosophical
debate. I could smell their unwashed clothing and the smoke
from their breath as their footsteps slapped in rhythm just behind me. I kept my eyes on the pavement and my pace steady
but quick, trying to hide my growing fear. Suddenly I felt the
arm of one man brush against mine. In a flash one man was on
each side of me.

Just as suddenly, they were in front of me, striding on
without so much as a pause in their conversation. But just as
they reached a sidewalk square ahead of me, one man spun
around and faced me. He took the cigarette butt out of his

mouth and said, "Sister, I just want you to know we're human beings, too. God loves us, and God loves you, and we love you, too."

Then he turned back, hurried on, and returned to the conversation with his friend. My skin tingled. I closed my eyes and let out a slow breath as the men moved on a few paces in front of me. One man swept his hand to the ground midstride, grabbed a cigarette butt from the dirt, and in one smooth motion lit it from his friend's and squeezed it between his teeth.

One block later, I reached my backpacker. As I stepped up the curb in front of the door, the men stopped again. "We just want you to know," one man said, "we were watching out for you." In a surreal conversation, one of the young men went on to tell me how they lived on the street. "See this scar," he said, pointing to a stripe across his nose. "I got this sleeping just over there. I woke up with a knife on my face and somebody stealing my shoes. He got the shoes, too." They talked on, not waiting for my response though I wouldn't have known what to say anyway. Before we parted, I stammered out a thank-you.

I want to go on expecting to find Jesus alive in dangerous alleys, at AIDS patients' bedsides, in crumbled school buildings, and in mud.

"Sister, it's nothing. We're not asking for money. We just want one thing," the guy with the scarred nose leaned forward, resting an arm on his friend's shoulder. "We want you to remember when you're waking up in your warm bed and going about your day doing whatever you feel like doing, remember we're here on the street. Just remember us."

I went upstairs and flopped down on the top bunk in my tiny backpacker cubicle, grabbed a pen and paper, and scribbled down everything I could remember from the day. Had I heard that man correctly? Were his words not the exact answer to my prayer? "We're human beings, too, and God loves us, and God loves you, and we love you, too." What kind of bizarre impulse made that young man say *that*?

I would never know what brought those words to his mouth. Maybe it was God dropping thoughts into his head that he didn't even understand. Maybe he had these kinds of conversations regularly.

Whatever brought those words to his mouth, I want to believe that there was more going on with him than what I first assumed. I want to believe Jesus Christ was as real and active in his life as in any pew I have ever sat in. I want to believe in the God who searched for sinners and sat with them, ate with them, listened to them, and showed them something worth believing in. I want to go on expecting to find Jesus alive in dangerous alleys, at AIDS patients' bedsides, in crumbled school buildings, and in mud.

True to the man's request, I remembered those men when I woke the next day and walked to my conference, feeling our Creator still watching over their shoulders and mine. I remembered them as I rode my motorcycle home to my family and my own double bed. I remembered them as I returned to the daily grind of recruiting young people to stay in school and start businesses in their rural homelands instead of fleeing to cities. As I write this now, I remember them, sleeping on the street, losing their shoes, feeling knife wounds across their young faces, and somehow, I hope, coming to know the God who also bore wounds out of love for them and for us.

QUESTIONS *for discussion and reflection:*

1. Why was the author exhausted by her experience at the conference? Why is serving in another culture often lonely?
2. How is it possible to "love your enemies" in dangerous situations?
3. How would you draw lines and make choices if you or your family were asked to serve in an area you considered dangerous?
4. The strangers told the author, "We're human beings, too. God loves us, and God loves you, and we love you, too." How should these words shape our attitudes for holistic mission work?
5. Read and reflect on Luke 6:20–22:

   Looking at his disciples, [Jesus] said, "Blessed are you who are poor, for yours is the kingdom of God. Blessed are you who hunger now, for you will be satisfied. Blessed are you who weep now, for you will laugh. Blessed are you when men hate you, when they exclude you and insult you and reject your name as evil, because of the Son of Man."

   How much time do you spend among people who are blessed by these standards (poor, hungry, weeping, or hated)? Why?
6. List three steps you want to take in the next month as a result of how this book has challenged you.

If you want to . . .

—participate in discussion forums on *Into the Mud*

—find links to volunteer opportunities and further reading

—see more photos of the people of South Africa

—communicate with the author

—and more . . .

Check out the *Into the Mud* website, www.intothemud.com.

ACKNOWLEDGMENTS

This book itself is a way of saying thank you to all the people in this book, for being the humble heroes that you are. I also want to thank the many more people around the world whose names do not appear in the book, but who have been integral parts of shaping this book and my life.

Special thanks to our old Bible study group, for those precious hours discussing the grit of life every Friday morning with many different accents, some tears, and plenty of warm beverages and hugs.

Thank you to the ever-smiling Sne for sharing your feet.

I am awed and blessed to have had such a thoughtful and caring editor as Madison Trammel. Thank you for noticing my proposal and believing in its potential.

Thank you to Drew, who earned himself a bag of jelly beans for nailing down the title, and who deserves far more than that for his ever thoughtful and gentle editing help. You chose well in marrying the lovely Leah, whom I also thank for being an encouragement and best friend ever since we sat in dorm rooms planning to live in mud huts together.

Thank you to many more editing helpers: Heather, who has the humility and wisdom to notice details like the fact that tigers do not live in Africa; Kevin, who has kept up the conversation that began years ago under the fine words of

Mr. Sider (what was he thinking!); Laura, who donated your amazing skills and expertise; Cory, who squeezed in time between rowdy football shorties and a needy baby; and Kara, who squeezed in time between that same needy baby and also has always offered a very precious friendship.

Thank you to Zeke and Phoebe for making me laugh and teaching me to love and being a part of "Mama's book."

I can never give enough thanks to my parents, for praying over my life and encouraging everything I have ever written (even back to that story I wrote in second grade about the bunny whose tail fell off), and for giving me unconditional love.

My enormous loving thanks to Adam, my biggest fan, photographer extraordinaire, spectacular amateur agent, and the love of my life without whom I would have long ago given up on this and many other creative endeavors.

And finally thank You to God, because everything worthwhile in this book is from You, and because the book is just a small piece of thank-You for all You do.

NOTES

Chapter 1—Noticing Things

1. John Updike, *More Matter* (New York: Alfred A Knopf, 1999), as quoted by Eugene Peterson, *Eat This Book* (Grand Rapids: William B. Eerdmans, 2006), 8.
2. Nasreen Seria, "Zimbabwean Inflation Surges to 11.2 Million Percent," *Bloomberg* (accessed 22 Aug. 2008). <http://www.bloomberg.com/apps/news?pid=20601116&sid=au8KvJA_Bwfc&refer=africa.
3. "Counting," *Weekend Witness* (July 26, 2008): 2.

Chapter 5—Open for Business: Nikiwe

4. Throughout this book, I have tried to use vocabulary that will invoke the right pictures for North American readers. I offer my apologies to South Africans who will find it strange to hear words like "minibuses" describing what they call taxis.

Chapter 6—The Good Soil: Madondo

5. World Bank, *World Development Indicators, 2007* (Washington, D.C.: World Bank, 2007).
6. United Nations Human Settlements Programme (UN-HABITAT). 2003. *Slums of the World: The face of urban poverty in the new millennium?*. Available on-line at: http://www.unhabitat.org/publication/slumreport.pdf. Nairobi: UN-HABITAT.

Chapter 7—Mixing and Mangling: Ernest

7. *Ingculaza* is hard for a nonnative speaker to pronounce, as the "c" in Zulu is a click like the sound of saying "tsk, tsk" to a child.
8. The "q" in Zulu is also a click, this one made by pulling the tongue away from the palette like the sound of popping open a bottle, so *Umvelinqanyi* is pronounced roughly, "Oom-vay-leen-kah-nee."
9. Louis J. Luzbetak, *The Church and Cultures* (Pasadena, Calif.: William Carey Library, 1970), 343.

Chapter 9—The Blooming Flower House: Charmaine

10. https://www.cia.gov/library/publications/the-world-factbook/geos/sf.html.
11. *2007 Sub-Saharan Africa 2007 AIDS Epidemic Update*, UNAIDS/WHO, 2008. See www.unaids.org or www.unaids.org or www.avert.org.

Chapter 10—Beautiful Language: Corina

12. The conversation in this chapter is reconstructed with Corina's permission almost entirely from exact quotes that I wrote down during future visits to her home.
13. South Africa has one of the most unequal distributions of wealth in the world, but in fact the United States is relatively unequal compared to other developed countries, with 29.9 percent of wealth in the hands of the richest 10 percent of the population. The globe as a whole has an even worse income distribution. Totaling all the incomes of the poorest 20 percent of the world's people comes to only 1.5 percent of the world income. Source: Michael Todaro and Stephen Smith, *Economic Development*, 10th ed. (Harlow, England: Addison-Wesley, 2009), 59, 228–29.

Chapter 11—Distant Voices: Sabelo

14. Pap is one of several names for one of Africa's most inexpensive foods, a sticky porridge made from cornmeal.
15. What South Africans call a taxi is more like what we would call a minibus. They are large vans or covered pickup trucks that fit a dozen or more people (sometimes *many* more).

Chapter 12—Remember Us

16. "South Africa Crime Stats," *Nationmaster* (accessed 24 Aug. 2008), http://www.nationmaster.com/country/sf-south-africa/cri-crime.

When Helping Hurts

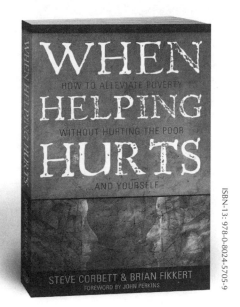

ISBN-13: 978-0-8024-5705-9

Churches and individual Christians typically have faulty assumptions about the causes of poverty, resulting in the use of strategies that do considerable harm to poor people and themselves. *When Helping Hurts* provides foundational concepts, clearly articulated general principles, and relevant applications. The result is an effective and holistic ministry to the poor, not a truncated gospel.

A situation is assessed for whether relief, rehabilitation, or development is the best response to a situation. Efforts are characterized by an asset-based approach rather than a needs-based approach. Short term mission efforts are addressed and microenterprise development (MED) is explored.

MOODY
PUBLISHERS
MoodyPublishers.com

The Missionary Call

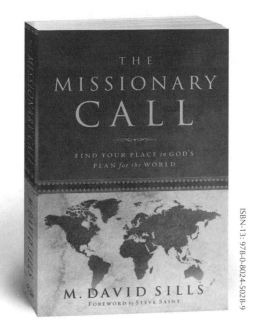

ISBN-13: 978-0-8024-5028-9

Christians of all ages recognize the heartbeat of God to take the gospel to the nations and wrestle with the implications of the Great Commission in their own lives. *The Missionary Call* explores the biblical, historical, and practical aspects of discerning and fulfilling God's call to serve as a missionary. Pointing the reader to Scripture, lessons from missionary heroes, and his own practical and academic experience, Dr. Sills guides the reader to discern the personal applications of the missionary call.

MOODY
PUBLISHERS
MoodyPublishers.com

Humanitarian Jesus

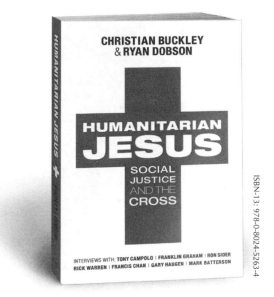

Throughout His ministry, Jesus cared for the poor, nurtured the sick and abused, and broke down social and racial barriers through acts of love and kindness. At the end of His ministry, Jesus commanded His disciples to "go and make disciples of all nations." Today's believers are called to heed Jesus' words and follow the example He modeled. Some believers, however, focus heavily on evangelism while others are heavily engaged in social justice. *Humanitarian Jesus* shows that evangelism and good works coexist harmoniously when social investment is subservient to and supportive of worship, evangelism, and discipleship.

MOODY
PUBLISHERS
MoodyPublishers.com